W9-CFM-053

KHW PLAIN AND SIMPLE SERIES

The

Choice

HYPOCRISY OR REAL CHRISTIANITY?

CHUCK & NANCY MISSLER

KHW

The Choice: Hypocrisy or Real Christianity?

Copyright 2001 by Nancy Missler

Published by The King's High Way Ministries, Inc.
P.O. Box 3111, Coeur d'Alene, ID 83816
www.kingshighway.org

First Printing, April 2001
Second printing, February 2010

ISBN: 978-0-615-34892-6

All Rights Reserved. No portion of this book may be reproduced in any form whatsoever without the written permission of the Publisher.

All Scripture quotations are from the King James Version of the Holy Bible (unless otherwise noted).

PRINTED IN THE UNITED STATES OF AMERICA

"Today I have given you **The Choice** between life and death, between blessings and curses. I call on heaven and earth to witness **The Choice** you make. Oh, that you would *choose Life*, that you and your descendants might live! Choose to love the Lord your God and to obey Him and commit yourself to Him, *for He is your Life*."

(Deut. 30:19-20, New Living Translation)

A Special Thanks

To Amy Joy Hess, for your wonderful examples, great stories and tremendous help.

To Mark and Debbie, for your labor of love, your great suggestions and your valuable time.

To Mandy, Nicole and Becky, for your prayers and help.

To Josh, Mark, Steve, Jim and Karen for reading the manuscript.

To Troy for your phenomenal editing skills. We will forever be grateful.

We thank God for all of you. (Philemon 4-7)

Table of Contents

Dedication

To Our Beloved Meshell,

You are the inspiration and the reason for the following pages; without you, this book would not have been written.

. . . Philippians 1:3

Introduction
Choose Life

I had never seen her before, but I will never forget her.

Her name was Lauren. She was about 19 years old, with beautiful long blonde hair, creamy skin and large, deep blue eyes. She reminded me of Cameron Diaz, with her vibrant smile and sparkling eyes. Even though I only met her one time, it was enough to make a lasting impression.

Lauren was the day nurse at a hospital I was visiting. She was so outgoing and friendly that we began to talk. She was in her last year of college and was headed to Costa Rica for five months to study to be a translator. She said it was important, not only to learn the language, but also to live in the country for awhile to achieve the proper dialect and become familiar with the culture.

I was so impressed with how she had taken hold of the direction of her life at such a young age. Truly, she had "life" all figured out and it was a delight to see.

I asked her how long she had worked at the hospital and she said, "about 11 months." Then she volunteered that working there had totally changed her outlook on living and dying. I questioned her as to how. She kind of groped around for the right words, and then simply came back to her original statement: it had "totally changed how she looked at living and dying." I thought perhaps she meant a changed spiritual outlook. So, I questioned her a little further and asked if she meant spiritually. "No," she immediately responded. "I tried that once and it really didn't work!" Then, she went on to explain why. She had gone to the same Christian church for most of her life, but unfortunately, many of her church friends *did not live what they preached.* There were some horrible conflicts. She ended up disillusioned and finally decided to drop the whole thing.

She said she was now happily into "karma."

(Her response really broke my heart.) I was saddened that this beautiful young woman, with so much to offer the world, had totally turned away from Christianity because of the actions of her so-called church-going friends. I was heartbroken because Lauren really believed that what she had seen in those people at her church, who "did not live what they preached," was *true* Christianity!

What's Real Christianity?

Authentic Christianity, however, is *not* what Lauren saw in those friends of hers. Real Christianity is not *saying one thing and doing another.* An *authentic* Christian is one who has the Life of Jesus showing forth in his actions, in his words and in all he does. He is not trying to "act like Jesus" or "say what He would say" or "do what He would do," but he is simply *choosing to let Christ live HIS Life out through him.* Real Christianity, therefore, is the moment-by-moment surrendering of *our lives*, so that *Christ's Life* can shine through.

Lauren's church-going friends are Christian phonies or hypocrites because they only *talk* about Jesus, but never really reflect His Life. (Many of us are doing the very same thing.) Now, it's not that we mean to be hypocritical or that we set out to be phonies, we don't! It's just that we don't know *how* to let Jesus live His genuine Life out through us. We're convinced that everyone else around us is living the "perfect" Christian life and we're the only ones having trouble. Consequently, we put up our masks a little higher and continue to "act like Jesus" in our own strength and ability, talking the talk, but certainly not walking the walk.

It's interesting that the two groups of people who recognize this phoniness, right away, are young people and non-believers. Others of us are fooled because we, often, are doing the very same thing.

Now, being a real Christian *does not* mean being "perfect" or "faultless," but simply knowing how to relinquish ourselves to God, so that He can live *His perfect Life* out through us. Thus, real Christianity is *not* rules, regulations and taboos. On the contrary, real Christianity is the most freeing and unrestricted way to live that there is!

That's what this little book is all about: how to be a real and authentic Christian and how this radically differs from being "religious" or "churchy."

My prayer is that this book will reach the "Laurens" of this world, and that through God's mercy and grace, they might come to know, not only what true Christianity is all about, but also that they might see the diametrical difference between real Christians and the phony counterfeits of this world. Thus, rather than be turned off by what they so often see in churches, they might, instead, be drawn to the real Creator of the Universe and the incredible freedom and Life that He offers.

John 10:10b tells us that, "...I [Jesus] have come that [you] might have Life, and that [you] might have it more abundantly."

This is God's promise to all of us!

How Did Phony Christianity Ever Begin?

How did we get so far from what God intended the Christian Life to be? What has caused the problem? How did this phony type of Christianity ever begin?

In order to understand the whole picture, it might be helpful if we go back to the very beginning...

In the Garden of Eden, everything was perfect. Adam and Eve genuinely knew God and they experienced His abundant Life. In fact, they knew God so well that He would often call out to them, come and visit them and fellowship with them. Then *sin* came: the choice *to live life as they pleased*, rather than live *as God designed*. When God called out to them after this, they *hid and covered themselves* with "fig leaves" because they knew they had quenched His Spirit (Genesis 3:7). At this point, all communion, fellowship and communication with God ceased and an impenetrable barrier was erected.

Ever since then, many have sought to repair and bridge the gulf between God and man, but to no avail. Man invented "religion" (rules and regulations in order to reach God) to address this void—*our own "fig leaves."* But, according to the Bible, "religion" has not been the answer. It has not worked. Rules and regulations can *never* bring us closer to God or pay the penalty for our sins.

God had His own way of fixing the breach between man and God, and *it wasn't religion.* Jesus, God's Son, was *not* religious. In fact, He was the most anti-religious person who ever lived. He continually hung out with the "wrong crowd," and attracted to His cause the "wrong types of people"—fishermen, prostitutes, tax collectors.

He was born in the Middle East, a Jew, and in Palestine, without the fanfare of a modern-day aristocrat. He didn't come to Washington D.C., or Salt Lake, or Moscow, or Rome, or Beijing, or Tokyo or London. He was born in Bethlehem, in the Middle East, before cars, planes, radios, TVs and even glass-bottom boats. The fishing boats of His day didn't have depth finders or swivel seats. In fact, if we were to see Jesus, Scripture tells us that He was a man of no esteem (Isaiah 53:3). He wasn't built like John Wayne or Tom Cruise; he was dark skinned, had a Jewish nose and probably was short. He was born in a manger, not in a hospital. The God of the universe didn't pack a North Face tent when He traveled. He didn't snap His fingers for dinner to magically appear; He simply started a fire and cooked His own fish.

Thus, God's way of fixing the breach between man and God was to send Jesus, His humble, yet radical own Son, to make peace between the world and Himself. Jesus came to earth and died in our place in order to save us from the penalty of sin (which is death) and to give us His Life. *Christianity is the only religion in the world where God Himself comes to dwell within each of our hearts.* All that is required of us is to reach up, confess that we can't make it on our own and take a hold of His hand. In other words, it's *His Life* that is offered, but *our choice* to receive it or not!

Thus, God's ways are *not* our ways. In fact, most of the time, God's way of doing things is completely opposite to the way we would do things. God isn't a bulldozer. He is ever so gentle, soft and comforting. Scripture even tells us that God loves us so much that He wants an ongoing personal relationship with us so that He *can* teach us individually *how to live Life as He designed.* In other words, He doesn't just call us to Himself and then drop us, He takes us even further by desiring to live His Life out through us. *This is what real Christianity is all about.*

Unfortunately, this way of living does not come about naturally, even for Christians! And this has been the big problem! As Lauren experienced, some Christians can often be unloving and unforgiving and frequently use God's Word like a club. These

Christians seem to find it easier to judge, criticize and be opinionated, rather than listen, lend a helping hand, love, serve and humble themselves before others, the way Jesus did. The latter describes a *real* Christian.

The Choice

Thus, as Christians, we are constantly faced with *The Choice* of: either living the Christian life in our *own* power and ability (like Lauren's friends); or, surrendering ourselves to God and letting *Him* live His Life out through us. One way leads to hypocrisy and phoniness, and the other to genuineness and real Christianity.

Again, most of us don't intend to be hypocrites or put on "fig leaves." It's simply that we don't know *how* to let Christ be our Life itself. We don't understand that as Christians we are *not* to try and "act" like Jesus, but simply relinquish our lives so that *He* can live His Life out through us. Also, because we don't know the difference between His Life and our own natural life, we don't recognize the times that we *are* phony. We can spot it in others, but seldom see it in ourselves. We know something is basically wrong, but we're unable to pinpoint the cause.

Thus, it's not by chance that you have picked up this little book, because God has a challenge for you. In Deuteronomy 30:19, He says: "Today, I have given you *The Choice* between life and death, and blessings and curses. I call on heaven and earth to witness *The Choice* you make. Oh, that you would *choose Life*, [so] that you...might live" (New Living Translation).

God's challenge is that you might *choose Life*—learn to let Christ live His Life out through you—and by doing so, you will live the abundant Life He designed! In other words, that you might experience *real* Christianity—life as He meant it to be!

If you are already a Christian, "choosing Life" means that God wants you to learn <u>how</u> to allow *His* Life (inside) in your heart to come forth and be your Life in your soul (outside)! If you are not sure where you stand with God, "choosing Life" means that He wants you to learn <u>how</u> to receive His Life into your heart so that you *can* begin to live Life as He designed.

Again, it's always *Jesus' Life*, but *your own choice* to accept it and then, moment by moment, pass it on.

Live Life as He Designed

Just like some of Lauren's "Christian" friends who only mouthed their faith, many of us do the very same thing. "Words" are so easy. The difficult part is living them out! God wants the Life of Jesus that He has *already* placed in our hearts, if we are believers, not just to remain in our hearts (and be words only), but to be shown out in our lives. He wants us to genuinely *live His Life*. Then, others will "see" God's abundant Life *in us* and *through us* and want what we have.

John 13:35 says, "By this shall all men know that you are My disciples, if you [truly] have Love one to another."

As we said before, *living Life as God designed* does not come naturally. It's only possible when we make **The Choice** to set ourselves aside and let God live His Life out through us. The question then becomes: *how do we do this*? What's the practical application of getting God's Life from our hearts out into our lives? If it doesn't happen automatically, then how does it occur? The answer is in the very next verse of Deuteronomy 30:20: by loving the Lord your God, by obeying Him and by committing yourself to Him, *for He is your Life*! In other words, if we learn to love God in the way that He intends, then we'll be able to live as He designed and have that abundant Life that He promises (Luke 10:28).

What Will You Choose?

How about you? What will you choose? Will you live Life as God designed or will you settle for a pale and phony imitation of Christianity, like Lauren's friends? Will your life make people run towards God or will it turn people away? God yearns that you might *choose Life*!

Choosing Life—*choosing to let Christ live His Life out through us*—is what this little book is all about. In these pages, we are *not* going to learn ways to "act like Jesus" or "talk like Jesus" or "love like Jesus," because *only* Jesus has the Life that we need and we can never *be* what only He *is*! What we will be learning, however, is *how to, moment by moment, make* **The Choice** *to love Him so that His Life from our hearts <u>can</u> shine through us and flow to others.*

It doesn't matter how long we have been Christians, how often we go to church, how many Bible verses we know or how sincere our prayers are, *authentic Christianity* is simply recognizing our own sin and self and then, choosing to surrender these things to God so that *He* can live His Life out through us. Again, it's His Life, but always our choice to give way to it.

God says in Matthew 7:14, "Strait is the gate, and narrow is the way, which leads to *Life*, and [only a] few will find it."

The question is: Will you be one who does?

The Key to "Choosing Life"

The *key* to letting Christ live His Life out through us, is the application of <u>four</u> truths and these will be the subjects of the following chapters.

1) First of all, learning *what Christ's Life really is* and how it radically differs from our own natural, human, self life. Learning how we can acquire God's Life in our *hearts* and how we can choose, moment by moment, to let it flow out into our own *lives*.

2) Learning that the foundation for living Christ's Life is knowing, without a shadow of a doubt, that *God loves us* with an unconditional and never-ending Love—a Love that is not based on *what we do* for Him, but simply on *who we are* in Him. This solid foundation is the only thing that will give us our security and identity in this life.

3) Learning what our own responsibility is in living Christ's Life—i.e., *learning to love God.* Learning, not only what quenches His Life and His Love in our hearts, but also how to make the appropriate choices to yield and surrender these things to Him.

4) And finally, learning how we can *pass Christ's Life along* to others. In other words, learning how to become cleansed and open so we can put their will and desires above our own. Only God can enable us to do this and this is only possible *after* we have learned to love Him.

Holy Masquerade

1) Underline up to three words that you believe best describe acts of hypocrisy by the average Christian?

Typical	Opposite	Honest
Self-righteous	Sinful	Rebellious
So!	Two-faced	Necessary
Sad	Fake	Selfish
Smart	Intolerable	Evil

2) Is it better to believe in Christ and not live the Christian Life, than to not believe in Christ at all? Write out your answer.

3) What do you think?

- Adults are more hypocritical than young people
- Young people are forced to be hypocrites by their parents
- The church should lower its standards so there would be less hypocrisy
- Most people do not see their own hypocrisy

4) How often do you live what you believe? Write your answer out.

5) Read each of the following verses and circle the one that comes closest to describing your life. Matthew 23:28, Romans 7:15-20, Galatians 5:19-21, Ephesians 4:22-24, Philippians 2:12-13, 1 Thessalonians 5:22.

Chapter One
What is Christ's Life?

Christian Hypocrites

Someone once said to me: "I'd rather not go to church anymore because they're all a bunch of hypocrites. They don't know how to really love. They all talk about it, but they sure don't live it. I work with 'so and so' (a church goer) and you should see what he does during the rest of the week! How on earth can he call himself a Christian? I don't want to have any part of it!"

Sounds like what Lauren encountered, doesn't it?

The Open Bible defines hypocrisy as "pretending to be something *we know* we are not." The word comes from the Greek theater. It's literally used of an actor, and means to "answer from under a mask." This means that the person recognizes the aspired goal or category—i.e., to be a good Christian—and pretends to be one, knowing all the while he is not.

The question: Can a Christian ever be guilty of this? *Absolutely!* Not only did Adam and Eve try to cover themselves and hide in Genesis 3:7, but six times in the New Testament, hypocrisy is talked about concerning Christians: Paul in Galatians 2 and James in James 5 are two examples. James 5:12 even warns the brethren that they not fall into *hypocrisy*. (This is not to mention the numerous times that Christ specifically speaks to the Pharisees about hypocrisy.)

Now, it's interesting because the two groups of people who seem to be able to spot phonies a mile away are young people and non-believers. We can't tell young people, "do as I say" and not expect them to look at our lives and see if it works for us. If it doesn't work for us in our lives, we can't expect them to want it either. *Our lives need to be examples of what we say, otherwise it's not the truth!* And this is the same kind of witness we need with our friends and our families. We need to live what we speak.

Now, it's not that we must be "perfect." No way! There is only One who is perfect and that's Christ. We simply must be running to Christ as the "answer" to all our problems, and by so doing, leading others to the only One who is perfect.

What's so tragic is that God must often, not only combat unbelief in a person, but also the damage other so-called Christians have done to them. The only thing that is ever going to truly touch another person's heart is seeing God's genuine Love and Life through us. Our flowery and empty words "about Jesus" are simply not enough. They need to see *a real changed life.*

An Example: "Supposed to be Like Jesus"

Joe was a brand-new Christian. He had come from a life of drugs, promiscuity and alcohol, but even in that circle he had many loyal friends. Now, these guys were not Christians, but Joe could always count on them. Thus, it was very difficult for him when he decided to move away to live with his aunt in another city. His aunt assured him, however, that she knew many young people at her church and that he would fit right in.

Joe's aunt was so delighted that he had finally become a Christian. She attended a church where half of the congregation was young people, and so she felt sure that Joe would be right at home. After years of praying for him, his aunt was so thankful that he was finally on the right track. Joe moved in with her, made new Christian friends and began attending her church. His aunt felt that, finally, she could relax. Joe was "home"!

But, not for long!

These new Christian friends turned out to be the "religious phony" types that we have been speaking about—Christians in name only. At first, they befriended Joe with open arms and included him in everything. They seemed so nice that Joe naively opened up and shared much of his background. That's all they needed. When Joe began to flounder and really needed the support of his new friends, that's when they turned on him. And, oh, how they flourished on the gossip!

One fellow who had befriended Joe early on, unexpectedly used all that Joe had confided in him as ammunition to control and manipulate him. Pretty soon, the whole church was buzzing about Joe. Poor Joe had made the mistake of trusting his new friends about his past because they were "Christians." He felt sure that "Christians" wouldn't talk. But, to his amazement and devastation, they did.

Joe was so crushed by this chain of events, that he decided to run back to his old ways. He determined to go, *not* because he missed the drugs or the booze, but because he missed friends who were loyal and "who really cared about him." He felt his old circle of non-believing buddies were a hundred times more true and more loving than these new "Christian friends."

Just before he left, he asked his aunt, "Tell me something. If people claim to be Christians, aren't they supposed to be like Jesus? Wouldn't *He* have kept my confidences? Wouldn't *He* have loved and comforted me when I was down? Wouldn't *He* have supported me no matter what? I thought Christianity was all about Christ's acceptance and Love. I guess I was wrong."

His aunt cried for three days!

Now, it's easy for us to judge others for being phonies and not loving as God desires, but we need to ask ourselves, "Am I being a phony too? Am I loving others any better than they are?" And, we need to be honest! In other words, we can't blame hypocrites for our own choices not to follow Christ. Each of us has to answer to Christ for ourselves. We have to obey God for ourselves and we can't use others as an excuse!

Another Example: Bumper Sticker Christian

A few years ago, we flew back to California late one Sunday night from a seminar in Washington State. Tired and hungry, we still had to face another one-hour drive home from the airport.

Trying to check out of the airport parking lot, we found at least 30 cars in the line ahead of us, moving very slowly. After sitting in the line for over 25 minutes, 10 or 15 cars from the very back of the line pulled out and went around the long line of waiting cars and tried to butt their way into the front of the line from the side aisles of the parking lot.

One big magenta truck jammed its way in front of us. We rolled down the window and politely said, "Please, you need to wait in line just like the rest of us." The man just laughed at us and jammed his big truck in front of us all the more. His kids were in the back of his truck and they, too, were laughing as he maneuvered his way in front of us.

To our complete disbelief, the man then stopped the whole line of cars behind him and let the 10 cars that had followed him, get into the line in front of him, adding another 10- to -15 minute wait for the rest of us. We were appalled that someone would be that self-centered and that rude. However, as we got closer to the lights and the checkout booth, we saw plastered clearly on the back of the big magenta truck, a Christian Ichthus (fish) symbol. We regret now that we didn't get out of our car and say to the driver of the magenta truck, "Is this is how a Christian acts?"

1 John 3:18 says it all, "Let us not love in word, neither in tongue [or stickers], but in deed and in truth."

Real Christianity

In the mid-1930s, a German pastor was handcuffed and taken from his church. Suspected of aiding Jews, he was immediately taken to prison and put in a five-foot cell. There was no hearing, no trial—not even time to let his family know what had happened to him.

For weeks, this gentle pastor asked the prison guard outside his cell door if he could use the phone at the end of the hall to call his wife and family and, at least, let them know he was alive. The guard, however, was a horrible man who hated anyone and everyone that had to do with Jews. He not only wouldn't let the pastor use the phone, he also determined in his heart to make the pastor's life as miserable as possible.

The sadistic guard purposefully skipped the pastor's cell when meals were handed out; he made the pastor go weeks without a shower; he kept lights burning in the pastor's room so he couldn't sleep; he blasted his shortwave radio hoping the constant noise would break the pastor; he used filthy language; he pushed him; he shoved him; and, when he could, he arranged for the pastor to have the most difficult job in the labor force.

The pastor, on the other hand, prayed over and over again not to let his hate for this guard consume him. He prayed instead to be able to forgive him and show him God's Love. As the months went by, whenever he could, the pastor smiled at the guard; he thanked him when his meals *did* come; when the guard was near his cell, the pastor told him about his own wife and his children; he even questioned the guard about his family and about his goals, ideas and visions; and, one time, for a quick moment, he had a chance to tell the guard about Christ and His Love.

The guard <u>never</u> answered a word, but, obviously, heard it all.

After months of unconditionally loving and giving himself over to this terrible guard, God's real Love and Life finally broke through. One night, as the pastor was again quietly talking to him, the guard cracked a smile; the next day, instead of his cell being skipped for lunch, the pastor got two; the following evening, he was allowed not only to go to the showers, but also to stay as long as he wanted; the lights began going off at night in his cell and the radio noise ceased. Finally, one afternoon, the guard came into the pastor's cell, asked him for his home phone number, and he, personally, made the long awaited call to the pastor's family.

A few months later the pastor was mysteriously released, with no questions asked.

This is an example of *real* Christianity! What happened to the pastor in the above story was supernatural. Naturally, he hated the guard and was certainly justified, by worldly standards, in doing so. But, the pastor loved Jesus more than himself, and thus he constantly made ***The Choice*** to let Christ live His Life out through him. Even though he had no human love left for the guard, Jesus did. And, that's all that mattered, because as the pastor surrendered himself, Jesus was able to pour His Love *through* him to the guard.

Houses Built Upon Sand

Letting Christ live His Life out through us might seem difficult at first, because it's totally opposite to everything we have ever been taught. It's like installing a brand-new foundation under a house. All is new! Once that foundation has been properly set, it's like a rock upon which everything else can be built.

Unfortunately, some of us older Christians have built our houses—our entire Christian lives—on quick-sand. We are born again, Jesus resides in our hearts and we love Him, but if we are honest with ourselves, we have lived most of our Christian lives in our own power and strength, and not Christ's. In other words, our foundation has not been Jesus at all, but "self." Thus, for many of us, God must jackhammer our existing foundations, tear down the walls of our houses, and then rebuild them all over again on new, solid foundations.

If you are just starting out in life, you are blessed, because everything—your whole spiritual life—is in front of you. Thus, hopefully, you can learn from the mistakes of others who have gone before you.

The Choice that will be continually before you: either to live the Christian life in your own power and ability and end up crashing and burning like so many other Christians you see today; or, learn to set yourself aside and let Christ live His Life out through you. The result of living the Christian life in your own power and ability is *hypocrisy* and, as Deuteronomy 30:19 says, "death and disaster." The result of letting Christ live His Life out through you is *real Christianity* and the genuineness and freedom that everyone is truly seeking. How we make this last choice is what this little book is all about.

What is Christ's Life?

How does Christ's Life differ from our own natural, human life?

God's Life, basically and simplistically, consists of three things: God's Love, His Wisdom and His Power to perform these things in our lives. Human life or self life, on the other hand, is the life we are born with and there is nothing supernatural about it. In fact, most of the time, it's completely contrary to what God desires. It consists of our own natural love, our own natural thoughts and our own natural power and abilities. These three natural elements are completely opposite to God's Life. God's Life is super-normal and comes only with the presence of Jesus.

Therefore, it's important to understand right from the start that God's Life and our natural, human life are completely opposite. Confusing these two things is one of the reasons why the Christian "church" is having such a difficult time.

Everyone has human, self life—we're born with it. Whereas, God's Life is a gift that we receive *only* when we ask Jesus Christ into our hearts to be our Savior. Therefore, *not* everyone possesses God's Life.

Now, of course, God loves us and is always reaching out to us and drawing us to Himself even *before* we become believers. But, in order to have the kind of Life that we have been speaking about here in this book—giving us the supernatural Love, Wisdom and Power of God—we must personally receive God's gift of Life, Jesus, into our hearts.

An Example: "Because Jesus is God!"

A perfect example of how Christ draws us to Himself is the wonderful story of Art Katz, a brilliant Jewish philosopher and professor at the University of California at Berkeley.

When Art came to the point in his life where he had accomplished all that he thought would bring him satisfaction, he still had this empty and unfulfilled feeling in his gut. He, thus, set out on a spiritual quest to find the real meaning of his life.

Art literally traveled all over the world in his search to find his true Messiah. While riding a train in

Germany, he happened to sit next to a young Christian girl who had only recently become a believer. They began to talk about God. A few minutes into the discussion, Art turned and sarcastically asked the young woman, "What makes you think your Jesus is any different from all the other religions in the world?" The girl looked at him lovingly and said, "Because Jesus is God. He is Love and He lives in my heart."

This response was *not* at all what Art had expected, and it caught him totally off guard. He could not argue with her from his intellect. For months, those ten simple words echoed in his mind... "Because Jesus is God and He lives in my heart."

Finally, Art found himself in Jerusalem, Israel. A Messianic Jew (a Jewish person who has accepted Christ as his Savior) befriended him and shared his own testimony. After experiencing tremendous love and compassion from this Israeli, the Holy Spirit broke down the walls of Art's heart and he, too, accepted Christ as his own personal Messiah. And, the God of the Universe, who is Love, just as that young German Christian girl testified, came to live in Arthur's heart.

How Do We Receive Christ's Life?

Asking Christ to become our Savior is the most important decision that we will ever make. But, we must recognize that it doesn't happen automatically. In other words, we are not born "Christians." *We must choose to become Christians.*

Again, it's Christ's Life that is offered, *but our own choice to receive it.*

How do we choose to receive the supernatural Life of God? We simply say, "Jesus I can't make it on my own. I keep blowing it. My life is a disaster. I don't know what I am doing or where I am going. I have fallen so short of what You wanted for me. I need Your Love and I need Your Wisdom and I need Your Strength. Please, come into my heart and be my life itself."

Romans 10:9-10 says, "...if you confess with your mouth that Jesus is Lord and believe in your heart that God raised Him from the dead, you will be saved. For it is by *believing in your heart* that you are made right with God, and it is by *confessing with your mouth* that you are saved" (New Living Translation).

By confessing these things and asking Him to come and be your very life, God will be faithful to hear your prayer, come and make His home in your heart and give you His Life.

Definition of God's Life

As we said, God's Life consists of three things: His Love, Wisdom and Power. In this little book, we will concentrate mainly on God's Love, with the understanding that all three of these attributes are always assumed. Sometimes, we may even interchange God's Life and God's Love, as they mean almost the very same thing. "God is Love" (1 John 4:12).

To define God's Life and His Love even further, let's read how God Himself describes it in 1 Corinthians 13:4-8:

"God's Love [His Life] is very patient and kind, never jealous or envious, never boastful or proud, never haughty or selfish or rude. God's Love does not demand its own way. It is not irritable or touchy. It does not hold grudges and will hardly even notice when others do it wrong. It is never glad about injustice, but rejoices whenever truth wins out. If you love someone [with God's Love] you will be loyal to him no matter what the cost. You will always believe in him, always expect the best of him, and always stand your ground in defending him. God's Love [His Life] never fails" (Living Bible).

In your own power and strength, can you live and love like this?

No way!

Try this experiment. Put your first name in place of the word "God" in the above Scriptures. For example, "*Nancy* is very patient and kind... never jealous or envious," etc. Now, read it out loud and see how it sounds. Pretty silly, huh? This graphically shows us how we can *never* be what God wants us to be on our own. It's only as we relinquish ourselves to Him and allow Him to live His Life out through us that these attributes can be ours.

Remember the pastor's story at the beginning of this chapter? It was only because he constantly surrendered his life to God that the Lord's Love and Life could come forth through him. Only God could have loved that guard. In the natural, the pastor's own love was dead because it was based on how he felt and what he thought. God's Love, however, continued to flow because it was based upon God and His faithfulness. And the same thing applies to us. No matter how we feel or what we think, no matter how another person responds to us and no matter what our circumstances are, God always has Love for that other person, even when we don't.

Christ's Life Through Us is not Automatic

It's critical, once again, to stress that God's Life through us does not happen automatically. Even though we are Christians and God's Life dwells in our hearts, we can still be full of "self": our own negative thoughts, wild emotions and self-centered desires. And if we don't choose to give these to God, they will quench God's Life in our hearts. In the above example, the pastor had a "legitimate" reason to hate the guard, but he knew that if he held on to that hate and unforgiveness, it would quench God's Life in him. Thus, he chose to yield all his thoughts and emotions that were "not of faith" and become that open vessel that God could use.

And, the same thing applies to us. We must constantly make *The Choice* to yield ourselves to God, so that He can pour His Life through us to others.

The point: God's Life in and through us is not automatic. It constantly depends upon our own choice, moment by moment. (If you want a *visual picture* of how this works, be sure to see "Supplementary Study" beginning on page 139.)

An Example: "You of Little Faith"

Charissa loved Jesus. Everybody who knew her could see it because He just bubbled out of her. When Charissa was 15, she and her older sister, Jesse, helped to start a youth ministry at their local church, and they both went every week. Even though Charissa was seven years younger than Jesse, Jesse often listened to Charissa's advice and wisdom because she knew it was from the true source: God. Because Charissa was abiding in God and constantly choosing His ways, God's Life just flowed through her and ministered to all those around.

One night as they were driving home from Youth Group, the two girls realized that they were nearly out of gas. They happened to be out in the middle of nowhere and miles away from any gas station. Jesse began to get nervous and begged God not to let them run out of gas, especially late at night. She prayed hard, but really didn't believe God would actually take care of them. She imagined having to walk and walk and walk and finally, ask someone for a ride to a gas station.

Charissa said to her, "Jesse, You of little faith!" Jesse didn't argue. Then, Charissa said, "Um... Luke 12:28." Jesse asked what Luke 12:28 was, but Charissa didn't know. So they looked it up. It was the passage that describes how God takes care of the ravens and the lilies, and says if 'He clothes even the grass which only lives for a day, how much more will he clothe you, O ye of little faith?"

Jesse couldn't believe it. Was that a coincidence? How did Charissa know that Scripture? She really didn't mind that God had told her she had little faith, because she knew it was true. Through this Scripture, He was gently telling them not to doubt Him; that He loved them; that He would take care of them; and that He would get them safely to a gas station. Which He did.

Later that year, however, Charissa got a job at a local mall, which required her to work on Sundays and Youth Group nights. With little Christian fellowship and support, Charissa started to lose her focus, and rather than recognizing it and continuing to make the right choices, she began to look elsewhere to fulfill her needs. She turned to a particular young man, Niles, who also worked in the mall. Slowly she began the slide downward, not recognizing that without the proper choices she couldn't remain as close to God as she had been. Eventually she even gave away her virginity—which she had promised God the year before never to give to anybody, but her husband.

Everybody who knew Charissa saw the change. They didn't know what the problem was or the reasons why, but the difference was obvious. Charissa lost her joy and the sparkle in her life. She became angry and frustrated and depressed. Now, when others shared their problems with her, like they used to, Charissa would respond with immediate criticism that showed no traces of love.

After many months, Charissa finally repented and made the decision to confess to her youth pastor and the rest of her family. By this time, however, she had become pregnant. Two years later, after many struggles with temptation and difficulties caused by the complications of having a child outside of marriage, Charissa returned to her place of abiding in God. She now helps lead the worship for the youth ministry at their church and she has God's Life, once again, radiating through her. She also has a beautiful little boy.....

Charissa learned the hard way, by "reaping what she sowed," that God's Life is not automatic. It takes work to constantly make *The Choice* to let Christ live His Life out through us. It's a daily decision.

Warning

Charissa's example, unfortunately, is all too common these days. Why?

Matthew 24:12 gives us some insight. This Scripture tells us that because many of our "spiritual" lives are built upon the sand (upon our own efforts and our own abilities and not God's), His Life in us has become quenched and blocked. Thus, as this Scripture says, "the Love of many [has grown] cold." And this is just what we are seeing.

Now, the interesting thing about this verse is that the Greek word for Love here is *Agape,* which can only mean God's supernatural Love. Thus, this Scripture is saying that in the end-times (just before

Christ returns) something is going to happen to the Love of God (or the Life of God) in Christians' hearts that is going to cause it to grow cold (or be quenched) in their lives. In other words, because these Christians will *not* be making **The Choice** to let God live His Life out through them, hypocrisy (or phony Christianity) will be the result. And this is exactly what we are seeing. Lauren's friends are examples.

What part can we play in turning the tide? It's obvious that we can't change others, as most of us have already tried. But, we *can* be open to learning God's "more excellent way" for ourselves and then, showing them by example, how it is done. Only real Christianity will bring others to a saving knowledge of Christ.

To Live Christ's Life Involves a Choice

We can't produce this kind of Life in our own strength or ability. To live God's Life is simply a matter of our will (or, our choice). It's saying, "Lord, I can't love this person in my own power. I don't even like them. In fact, I can't stand them right now. But, Lord, I know that You love them and will give me the Love that I need. So, I choose to relinquish my "self" (my own thoughts, emotions and desires that are contrary to Yours), so that Your Life (Your supernatural Love, Wisdom and Power) can shine through me." In other words, I *Choose Life*!

Thus, to live God's Life is *not* dependent upon how we feel or what we think. It's simply letting God

Himself live His Life through us. God is the One doing the loving and the living, not us, and all that He requires from us is *The Choice* to allow Him to do so. Thus, only *our will* is involved in the choice, not our emotions or our thoughts. This is, again, demonstrated in the story about the German pastor. Even though the pastor didn't feel like it or want to, he chose, by faith, to allow God to use him to show His Love. And, of course, God was faithful to do so.

Matthew 26:39 tells us that God has given us the authority and the power to continually say, "Not as I will, but as Thou wilt." This way of responding, however, is completely opposite to the way we normally would respond, which is usually based upon how *we* feel and what *we* think. What we "feel" and what we "want," is usually what we "do." However, when we learn God's way of Life and make *The Choice* to say "not my will, but Thine," God will be faithful to pour His Life through us, enabling us to do His will. (See "Supplemental Study," page 162 for a *visual picture* of this.)

Again, it's His Life, but always our continual choice to surrender to it.

An Example: "It Blew Her Away!"

Here's an example that shows the power of our choices. Kristin, the 19-year-old daughter of a pastor and his wife, was caught sleeping with her boyfriend. Kristin's mom was absolutely horrified when she found out, but even worse, she was afraid to tell her husband for fear of what he would do. He was totally rigid about this sort of thing.

After a while, however, the mom realized that she couldn't handle the situation all by herself and knew she had to tell her husband. She called him at church and told him everything. Just as she had imagined, he blew up and determined to come home right then, confront Kristin, forbid her to see her boyfriend again, kick her out of the house and take away her car.

Fortunately, the mom had been learning about *The Choice* that we, as Christians, continually have to make: either to live God's Life or our own. Thus, she knew that if the two of them reacted out of their own anger and hurt, the situation would probably get worse. Believing that God had the perfect solution, the mom prayed and asked God to soften her husband's heart. God did just that, because when he arrived home that night, she was able to convince him that they mustn't confront their daughter in anger. The pastor repented of his own critical attitude and together they went before the Lord. They gave all their disappointment, anger, frustration and bitterness to Him and chose to handle the situation as the Lord would want.

They waited up for Kristen, met her at the door and lovingly asked if they could talk. First, they shared their own hurt in finding out what she had been doing, and then they shared how grieved God must be, since He loved her far more than they ever could. Continually, they kept the emphasis on themselves and on God, without pointing fingers at Kristin.

Kristin immediately felt God's Love pouring forth through her parents, convicting her that what she was doing was wrong. And, because it was God's Love, she reacted from her heart, not her emotional defenses. She broke down sobbing and after awhile, repented not only to her parents, but also to God, asking His forgiveness. In the end, the entire family was reunited.

Kristin later shared that before meeting with her parents, she had determined to move out of the house because she knew what her dad's reaction would be. But, when she saw his genuine Love and concern that night, she said it blew her away! "It was like the very presence of God in that room tearing down all my defenses and exposing my sin."

This is an example of real Christianity!

Note something interesting about this story: When it's God's Life *through us* and not our own emotional outbursts, it will not only prompt a contrary-to-normal action on the part of the one showing love (i.e., no expectations or presumptions), but it will also prompt a contrary-to-normal response on the part of the one being loved (i.e., responding from his heart, not his defenses). In the above example, the dad (the lover or the initiator) acted differently than he normally would because of God's Love *in him,* and Kristin (the one being loved) responded differently than she had intended to because of God's Love *to her.*

God is the light that exposes the heart of the one being loved and that light will either cause him to draw closer to God, as in the above example, or it can cause him to flee and hide. It's a very powerful thing to stand naked in front of a Holy God, totally exposed by His light and many people just cannot bear this and often, will run. In most cases, however, if the one loving continues to reach out and continues to love as God designed, the end result will be that the relationship will be healed. Again, the German pastor's story is an example. He continued to love that guard, in spite of his responses. Finally, God's Love and Life tore down the walls in the guard's heart and a relationship resulted.

God tells us in 1 Corinthians 13:8 that His Love will never fail!

His Life in Us Proves We Are Real Christians

Again, the Bible tells us that others will know we are Christians, not by our words, our knowledge of Scripture or our spiritual gifts, but simply by showing God's real and genuine Life and Love (John 13:35). In other words, we prove we are Christians only when we live as God designed.

When we live in this way, people will be drawn to us, not only because of the freedom we experience *to be ourselves*—the freedom to be real and genuine and yet still show forth Christ—but also the freedom we give them *to be themselves*. Someone recently told me, "This is the first time in years that I have begun to like who I really am, and what God is doing in my life. I am finally free to be who I really am, and you know what? It's not bad at all."

An Example: Hell's Angel

Here's a great example of someone who yearned to be free to be himself, and yet still show forth Christ.

Years ago, in Tasmania, Australia, there was a member of the Hell's Angels named Al, who was in a situation where he was about ready to kill a man. Now, I'm not sure of all the details, but miraculously, someone stopped him from doing so and, afterwards, shared Christ with him. Al seemed open, so the person gave him one of *The Way of Agape* tapes. Through this little tape, Al came to know Christ as his own Messiah.

God's ways are certainly not our ways. That tape was done by a Southern California housewife who was struggling in her marriage. But, somehow, the Spirit of God sent that tape all around the world and used the words shared to minister to a hardened Hell's Angel gang member down in Tasmania, Australia. Truly, God does choose the foolish things of the world to confound the wise (1 Corinthian 1:25).

Al said later that the thing that drew him to the Gospel message was the freedom it talked about to be "who we really are" and yet still reflect Christ. This really spoke to his heart and he wanted that more than anything else in the world.

Al began to study God's Word and *His* way of Life. Eventually, he reconciled with his own wife and family, and began a church for "bikers" like himself.

The last time we visited Tasmania to do a seminar, Al showed up to meet us. He was tall, good looking and dressed in black leather with chains dangling everywhere. When he first saw us, he ran towards us, lifted us up in his arms and swung us around like rag dolls. We loved him instantly. He truly was a free man! Free not only from his past, but also free to live and love as God designed—free to be himself, and yet, show forth Christ! Isn't that what we all want?

How wonderful it is to live without masks and facades, where what we are thinking and feeling on the inside is exactly what is showing on the outside! It's not that we won't have bad days, we will. We're human. But, even in those difficult times, if we make the right choices to surrender ourselves to God, we can still show *His* Life in spite of our circumstances.

The world is desperately looking for this kind of freedom. We as Christians, more than anyone else, should be showing others how to obtain it. We have the answer...it's Christ in and through us. However, if we *don't* make *The Choice* to let Christ live His Life out through us, then we'll, once again, end up those Christian hypocrites turning more people away from Christ than bringing them to Him.

The Ultimate Question

As believers, God has given us the awesome responsibility of showing forth His Love and His Life to a very needy and dying world. The question is: Have you *Chosen Life*? Are *you* living this kind

Chapter Two
The Only Foundation

Building Our Houses on the Rock

We began this little book talking about houses—spiritual lives—that are built on "sand" and how they crumble at the first hint of a storm. What we'd like to explore now is how we can make sure our house is built on the "rock" so that when the tests come, it will withstand the onslaught. It's not enough to accept Christ into our lives, we must also have an on-going love-relationship with Him, so that we are assured of His personal Love.

Many of us, in our haste to be "like Jesus," have forgotten the first basic step of Christianity, which is to know for ourselves the extent and the depth of God's Love. If we really knew how much He loved us, there would *never* be any reason for us to fear what He might allow into our lives. If we really knew how much He loves us, we would have the confidence and the trust to continually abandon our lives into His care and know that, no matter what our circumstances are, He will be there.

Thus, before we can go any further in learning how to let God use us as an open vessel, we *first* need to know that we are loved by the Father. Once we are assured of this, then we'll have the confidence to continually surrender our wills and our lives to Him. In other words, knowing that God loves us is the foundation of our faith. Without knowing this, we won't be able to move forward in our Christian walk. We can't lay our lives down to someone and love them if we really don't think that they first love us. This principle is true no matter how long we have been Christians, no matter how many Scriptures we know or how many Bible studies we attend.

If we know that God loves us, then we'll be able to, daily, see His handprint of Love in all that we do. If we doubt His Love, we'll not only limit ourselves from experiencing His personal touch, we won't experience His Life and Love for others. Now, this does not mean that God is not still in our hearts, loving us. He is! It just means we *won't* have that daily, living experience of seeing His Love at every turn. (See *visual picture* of why this occurs on page 165 in "Supplemental Study.")

Knowing God Loves Us Unconditionally

God tells us in His Word that we are loved, special and of inestimable worth in His eyes, not because of what we *do*, or what we don't do, what we look like or what we don't look like, but simply because we are His children. Period! We are His kids and He is going to continue to love us regardless of how many mistakes or how many failures we make. He loves us *unconditionally* and *never-endingly*. Thus, whether we are at home relating to our family, or at school with our friends or in the business place, God loves us—with no strings attached! When we really know this—experientially know this—it gives us the freedom to relax and just be ourselves. God loves us and He loves us just as we are! What hope this gives us to weather anything that might come into our lives.

We must understand that nothing, *absolutely nothing*, can ever separate us from the Love of God in our hearts. Even our waywardness, our fears, our unfaithfulness, our doubts and our disobedience won't stop God's Love from coming. His Love is unconditional. Nothing can alter or stop it.

As Romans 8:38-39 says, "For I am persuaded, that neither death, nor life, nor angels, nor principalities, nor powers, nor things present, nor things to come, nor height, nor depth, nor any other created thing, shall be able to separate us from the Love of God, which is in Christ Jesus our Lord."

An Example: "Beauty for Ashes"

Drew gave his life to Jesus when 12 years old, and he grew rapidly in the Lord. When he was 14, however, the uncle who had been his spiritual mentor died. With little spiritual grounding, Drew fell away. He became involved in several physical relationships with girls, and was also drawn into a relationship with a full-grown man in the town. He could not get out of this homosexual relationship. Being much older and smarter, the man was able to manipulate Drew and force him to keep returning, even though Drew hated it and hated himself. When he was 16, he was finally big enough to stand up for himself, and though he never went back, the emotional, spiritual and psychological damage was enormous, and thus he slid deeper into all sorts of self-destructive behavior.

When his girlfriend gave birth to a son, Drew's dad told him he had to marry her. Marriage, however, did not stop his behavior. He had been running drugs up and down the east coast and partied often. He drank heavily and often cheated on his wife. After his first marriage fell apart, he took another man's wife, and married her once his divorce was settled.

Hardly a month after the wedding, Drew was diagnosed with drug-induced hepatitis, which made him very ill. A number of accidents smashed up his body, including a severe motorcycle wreck and being knocked 14 feet by the bucket of a backhoe. He took care of the pain by taking even more drugs, both legal and illegal. He used alcohol as an excuse. He could say, "I'm an alcoholic" and that got people off of his back about making responsible choices.

All during these years, Drew grew to hate himself to the point where he didn't care if he lived or died. He scared other men in fights because they saw that he just didn't care. He didn't care if he killed them and he didn't care if he was killed. God cared however.

Finally, Drew just couldn't stop himself from doing things that he despised. When a woman would proposition him, he couldn't say "no." He was like a dog that any woman could lead around. He hated it, but felt he had no power to stop himself. He tried drug rehab, A.A. and prayer. He was desperate for God or someone to do something.

Finally, one day, he and his daughter were driving down a winter road, and they hit a patch of ice and spun out. His air-bag inflated when they bounced off a tree stump, but deflated by the time they hit the cliff wall. The seatbelt stopped him so fast that the only thing that kept his already-damaged neck from snapping, was that his face smashed into the windshield. The extent of Drew's injuries was immense. He received serious wounds and bruises on his face and in his mouth, and had to have his jaw reconstructed and wired shut for nearly a year. His daughter left the accident unharmed.

That did it. Laid up again, Drew spent hours every day reading God's Word. God made it clear to Drew in the hospital that He loved him and that He had saved his life. As Drew learned, more and more, to abandon his life into God's hands, the weight of sin and incredible shame and pain that had held him bound for so many years, lifted. One day, two years later, Drew felt the awesome power of God move upon him, and he experienced the completeness of the forgiveness that God had already given him. The abundance of God's Love worked wonders in the demolition zone of Drew's heart, and he truly became a new man, full of confidence in the power of God and His healing, cleansing and abounding Love.

An amazing set of events followed. Drew's marriage fell apart in spite of his repentance and incredible turnaround. His wife still divorced him, and refused to let him see his four daughters. In spite of this, he never had another case of infidelity.

Women still approached him, but he found it easy to refuse them. He became free from alcohol, drugs and even cigarettes, and in God's power, completely stopped taking any kind of pain medication. His liver problems also subsided and he testifies that he feels better now than he did when he was a teenager. Those around him see God continuously answering his prayers. In recent months, God has even opened the doors for Drew to see his children again and to start being the father they desperately need.

Another answered prayer is that the Lord eventually brought Drew a lovely Christian bride who is more than he could ever have dreamed of or hoped for. She and Drew are the best of friends, lovers and make wonderful partners in ministry.

God picked Drew up out of the pit and has given him "beauty for ashes, the oil of joy for mourning, the garment of praise for the spirit of heaviness; that he might be called a tree of righteousness, the planting of the LORD, that HE might be glorified" (Isaiah 61:3).

The most important thing for us to know, as we learn to let Christ live His Life out through us, is that God loves us. He loves us unconditionally and unendingly, no matter how badly we blow it. Always remember Drew's story. If God can forgive him and love him, He can do it for any of us! If we really know and understand this, then we'll be able to continually yield ourselves to Him so that He can pour His Life and His Love through us to others. If we are unsure of His Love, however, then when things go badly, we'll jump to the conclusion that He really doesn't care and that He doesn't love us. And, consequently, we'll close ourselves off to His Life.

Isaiah 43:2-4 states, "When thou passest through the waters [trouble], I will be with thee; and through the rivers, they shall not overflow thee: when thou walkest through the fire, thou shalt not be burned: neither shall the flame kindle upon thee. For I am the Lord thy God...Thou wast precious in My sight... and I have loved thee..."

Another Example: "She Sang Like An Angel"

Sandy was a young Christian girl in her early twenties who had a very troubled background: drugs, alcohol, homosexuality, abuse, etc.

When Sandy came to a women's retreat in the mountains, she had told God, "You have to show me this weekend that You really love me or I can't go on." She had become so disillusioned with her life, her friends, her church and her family, that she decided if God didn't really love her, she wanted "out." Sandy begged God to somehow show her this particular weekend that He really cared. She told Him that if she didn't see or hear something from Him, then she was going to take matters into her own hands.

Saturday afternoon, the second day of the retreat, Sandy walked the grounds of the camp, contemplating how she was going to end her life. She passed by another young woman, Pat, who sensed

Sandy's despair, but didn't say anything because she was intimidated by Sandy's harsh countenance.

That evening communion was held. Sandy, by this time, was totally despondent. Out of desperation she told God that she was going to refuse communion until He somehow showed her that He loved her. After everyone had taken communion and left the auditorium, Sandy moved from her seat up to the communion table. She quietly knelt down in front of the table, and put her head down on her folded arms. She determined to stay there until somehow she felt God's Love.

After she had knelt there for almost an hour, the doors in the back of the auditorium opened and someone came in. Sandy couldn't see who it was because of the L-shaped room. This person quietly moved over to the fireplace and began to sing in the Spirit. Sandy still couldn't see who it was, but she said later that this woman "sang like an angel."

Sandy kept her head on the communion table for at least a half hour more. The woman at the other end of the building continued to sing. Finally, Sandy couldn't stand it any longer, and came around the corner to see who was there. The young girl singing was Pat, the one she had passed that day in the garden. Pat seemed startled at first, but then in an authoritative voice, told Sandy, "Sit down, God told me to come to you." Absolutely shocked, Sandy sat down and they began to share.

The Lord had laid Sandy heavily upon Pat's heart all weekend. But, because of Sandy's attitude,

Pat had kept her distance. After the Saturday night communion, Pat had retired to her cabin and gone to bed. She was almost asleep when God prompted her to get up and to go minister to "someone who needed Him in the main sanctuary." Never dreaming it was Sandy, Pat, at first, rolled over and tried to ignore the Holy Spirit's voice, but because no peace would return, she finally got up, put on her robe and obeyed.

When she arrived in the auditorium, no one was there. But the Lord made her stay, wait and sing. When Sandy finally did appear, Pat said at first she was scared to death. But, she gave her fear to God and He told her what to say. The two women shared all night long. They cried, they hugged and they laughed. God, in His unfathomable way, had shown Sandy (through His angel Pat) how much He loved her.

The next morning, both girls got up in front of the entire audience and shared what had happened. There wasn't a dry eye in the entire auditorium.

Pat is an example of *real* Christianity!

A Gift of Love

God's Love is not only unconditional, it is also "a gift." His Love is translated *charity* in the original King James Version of the Bible, which means "unconditional Love in action." God's Love is a Love that originates in the heart of God and keeps on coming, even when the object of that Love refuses to reciprocate or accept it. The significance of the word charity is that it is *a gift of love with no strings attached*. Here's a perfect analogy:

Many years ago, there was an article in the *Los Angeles Times* that told the story of a nine-year-old girl who was flying from England to the United States to have a kidney transplant. The girl's parents had raised all they could toward the operation, but had managed to raise only $7,000, far short of the $30,000 needed.

The people on the flight from England to the United States somehow heard of the little girl's situation. Unconditionally, they began to give of themselves all they could; men gave watches, cash, and checks. One man wrote a check for $10,000. Women gave rings and any other jewelry they had. The people on that plane raised an amazing $23,000! That, plus the $7,000 the parents had raised on their own made the exact amount needed.

The neat thing about this story is that the little girl's nationality, her religion or her social status didn't matter to the people on that plane. They didn't say, "Well, let's see, I will lend you this money, but you must pay it back." No. They simply gave all they could give *with no strings attached.*

This story reminds me of God's Love, because His Love does exactly the same thing. He unconditionally gives Himself over to us with no strings attached. He loves us even when we cease to please Him and even when we try to stop His Love from coming.

Hollywood-Type Love

If we don't understand what God's Love really is, then we'll get confused, thinking it's the same as human love, and we'll continue to have the same problems as before.

Here's a letter that describes our "traditional" view of love:

During my teen years, I read tons of trashy "love" magazines and novels. I was a movie addict and later, a TV addict. As a result of all this garbage, I had a very difficult time with the concept of God's Love. It wasn't so much that I didn't believe that God loved me, it was more that I hadn't a clue as to what real love was! I really thought it was about making me "happy" and "feeling good about myself and my life." By Hollywood standards, if someone "really loved you," they gave you whatever you wanted and made you "happy."

We've been brainwashed into thinking the Hollywood version is the correct version. And, when we begin to look for this kind of love from God and it doesn't happen, we assume that He doesn't love us or, at the very least, we become confused. In the movies, you do 1, 2, 3, 4 and boom— instant love. But, when we try that "instant" formula with God, it always bombs. Therefore, the logical conclusion we come to is either God doesn't love us, we are unlovable or He doesn't exist.

I think there are probably a lot of kids still being raised on that Hollywood type of love just like me. What is so sad is that what they are learning is so distorted and so incorrect that it will almost certainly make their lives very difficult. Many, I know, won't be able to get past that dream of, "we are entitled to love and happiness." After all, many of our mom's told us so.

And then we wonder why there are so many broken relationships, split churches and severed marriages today. Many of our shattered dreams were put there by "Hollywood's version of love."

How Does God Communicate His Love to Us?

God cannot be boxed in and He will manifest His Love in each of our lives as He so desires. Some of the ways that He communicates His Love to us is through reading His Word, through other people, through confirmation of His Spirit and through our circumstances.

One of the surest and most visible ways that He lets us know how much He loves us is by our daily reading of His Word. This is where it all starts. This is how God talks to us, and this is how we hear His Voice. As we read His Word, we must choose, by faith, to believe what He is saying. Then, we can step out in faith, knowing that in His timing He will align our feelings to match what we have chosen to believe. It all begins, however, with reading and believing His Word.

Often, when something difficult happens in our life, we need a "word" from the Lord just to confirm that He is still there and that He still cares. Nothing means more to our hearts than when we pick up our Bibles, and there in our daily reading is just the perfect thought that validates how much God loves us.

For instance, a friend of mine complained that she had too many things going on in her life and was really stressed about it. She made a list of all the things that she was involved in, prayed about them and asked God to show her which ones she was to drop. Her list read: Bethel Ballet, Bible Studies, wife, mother, etc. (not necessarily in that order!).

In her daily reading the very next day, she got Joshua 16:2, which says, "Goeth out from Bethel." Just a coincidence, right? I don't think so. The next day, she received several other confirmations from the Word that confirmed it was God speaking and that He *did* want her to drop out of her Bethel Ballet classes. Her husband concurred and, after she had dropped the class, her peace returned.

Another way that God often communicates His Love to us is by experiencing His Life in place of our own. When we experience His Love for a person we know we're unable to love in our own ability, it proves to us that God must love us. When we experience His Power getting us through circumstances we know in our own strength we couldn't manage, it proves that He really cares. And when we experience His Wisdom shedding light in an area we know we didn't understand before, it proves that God is intimately concerned about every detail of our lives. Experiencing His Life in place of our own is something that will convince us, more than anything else, that God is real, and that, yes, He does love us.

Remember John 10:10b, which states, "...I [Jesus] am come that they might have life, and that they might have it more abundantly."

Another way that God communicates His Love to us is through our own personal circumstances. There's nothing quite so comforting as knowing that God's hand has personally orchestrated every detail of our lives. It's a constant reminder that He does, indeed, love us. Following are a few examples.

Candy: "A Day I Will Never Forget"

When Candy was 18, she broke her leg. Through the post-op examinations, she was diagnosed as having bone cancer. After eight weeks of chemotherapy, her leg was amputated. Several more months of chemo followed, as did the loss of her hair, her job, her independence and the illusion that she would live to be an old woman with no serious health problems.

She had already been a Christian for about four years, so she was well-grounded to begin to rebuild her life. She finished her college education, moved out of her parents' home and began to earn a master's degree in clinical psychology. She had a lot of faith that God would bless her with a job in line with her new training as a therapist. But, as time went by and no responses came to her resumes, she started to question God. "Maybe I got the wrong degree...maybe I won't find a job...maybe I'll have to give up my own apartment and move in with my parents again..." What began as a small worry quickly escalated into sheer panic.

Then the most amazing thing happened. As she sat in her dining room, with tears streaming down her face, turning all these questions over in her mind, she heard a clank in the living room. She stopped crying, wiped the tears from her face and went to investigate. She had her cassette holder screwed to the wall with about 40 cassettes neatly placed in slots. The noise she heard was caused by one of those tapes falling out of its slot (just the one) and crashing onto the floor. This was odd, because there was no jolt, no movement of any kind in the room, and yet this one tape flew out.

She picked up the cassette from the floor and noticed that it was run part way through. She put it into her stereo player just as it was, and hit the PLAY button. What she heard on that tape was exactly what she needed to hear at that very moment. The portion of the message, beginning right at the spot where the tape had been stopped, was all about how much God loved her. It shared how everything in her life was permitted by the Father for a reason and a purpose, and that nothing had happened accidentally; all was orchestrated by His Love. The teaching also went into the importance of personally knowing how much He loves us, *before* we are able to give ourselves totally over to Him. It said something to the effect, "Do you know why you don't have faith that God is going to take care of you? Because you don't understand how much He loves you...."

Candy really believes that an angel knocked that tape off the wall to personally deliver a message that she desperately needed to hear at that exact moment—God loves her! Nine days later she was hired as a counselor by a huge California medical institute called Hospice Care. She said it was a "dream job" and a total blessing.

Candy says she will "never forget that day" and cherish the memory of God's infinite Love and caring.

Nancy: "His Name is Clifford"

My Chuck travels extensively.

In the middle of the night several months ago when he was gone, I heard something in our house. Now, I didn't hear enough to call the police, but I heard enough to be scared to death and unable to go back to sleep.

As I lay there, I began to think that what I really needed was a good LARGE "watchdog," one who would alert me to the fact that someone was on my property before they were able to get into my house. The next morning, after searching the house and finding nothing, I thanked God that He protected me, and then I began to pray. In my prayer journal, I wrote: "Lord, if it be Your will, I would really like a large watchdog, and yet, he must be super gentle with all my grandbabies (I have two that live on our property). I'd like a dog that is young enough to get along with all our other animals, yet who is completely housebroken and over the chewing stage. He must be a male, and yet I'd like him to be shorthaired." I gave the list to the Lord and asked Him that only His will might be done.

Later that morning, I called my daughter and told her about the incident. She suggested we go immediately to the humane society and see what dogs they might have. On the way there, we tried to explain to my three-year-old grandson, Noah, why Grandma needed a watchdog. Out of the blue, he said, "Grandma, you need a Clifford!" Now, at the time, I had no idea what a "Clifford" was! So, my daughter promptly explained that "Clifford" is a series of children's books about a large red dog.

When we got to the shelter, we showed the lady in charge my detailed "want" list: "a large male watchdog, yet one that is gentle and tender; a puppy, yet one that is housebroken and beyond the chewing stage; a male, yet one that is shorthaired, etc." She smiled and said, "Rather a hard bill to fill, wouldn't you say? But, there is one dog here that fits that description perfectly and his name is *Clifford*!

That very night I had a large, male, shorthaired, red (and white) watchdog (with a ferocious bark), but who adores Noah and babies; he is six months old, but fully housebroken, sleeping at the foot of my bed protecting me. He's absolutely perfect! He's a love-gift sent directly from God, and when I look at him, I remember how much God loves me.

Now, we can't always depend upon our circumstances alone to tell us if God loves us or not, because often He will use our situations to test us and to help us grow in our faith. But, when we read about His Love in the Word, feel it through our brothers and sisters, His Spirit bears witness of it and our circumstances confirm it; then we can be sure that what we are seeing and hearing is God's voice of Love.

Diana: "A Bird's Nest"

One of the most beautiful examples of someone who knew, without a shadow of a doubt, that God loved her was a young 28-year-old woman named Diana Bantlow.

Diana had only been a Christian for two years when she was diagnosed with leukemia and given only six months to live. No matter how much pain she was in or what she thought or felt, Diana continually *chose* to abandon herself into God's care, because *she knew that He loved her*. She knew He wouldn't allow anything into her life that He hadn't personally permitted or that wouldn't eventually bring Him glory.

She was invited to teach a Bible study those last six months of her life. Many times, she would come to teach us after her painful chemotherapy sessions. We would prop her up on the sofa, prop pillows around her, and she would begin to tell us about God's Love and His faithfulness and His trustworthiness.

Of course, there wasn't a dry eye in the whole room. She had an intimacy with God like no one I had ever seen before.

Diana's leukemia was diagnosed in June, and by November she was permanently confined to the hospital. At Thanksgiving, I wanted to give her something to show her how much I loved her and how much she had ministered to my life.

That particular weekend, however, my three-month-old daughter Michelle was ill, and I needed to run to the pharmacy to pick up her medication. I thought it would also be a perfect time to get something for Diana. In the car I prayed and asked God to point out that gift that "He had in mind" to communicate His Love to her. I got the prescription, and on the way out of the pharmacy I noticed a cute bird's nest, all done in fall colors with two little sparrows in it. I just knew it was for Diana. I quickly bought it and raced home.

On the way home, I looked down at the little bird's nest in my lap and began to wonder about its appropriateness. I asked God, "Is this really what You had in mind for Diana? A bird's nest?" The Scripture that immediately came to me was Matthew 10:29-31, "Are not two sparrows sold for a farthing? And one of them shall not fall on the ground without your Father. But the very hairs of your head are all numbered. Fear ye not therefore, ye are of more value than many sparrows."

Well, I was excited because it fit so perfectly. So, I wrote it on a card, put it with the nest, and asked Chuck when he got home to deliver it to the hospital for me.

About a half an hour later, Diana called and said, "Oh Nancy, I love the bird's nest! I know it's from God because He always tells me not to fear! But," she said, "what you don't know, and what no one else knows—except for God—is that because of the chemotherapy, I am losing all my hair. And God tells me right here that *He loves me so much that 'all the hairs on my head are numbered' to Him."*

That's our faithful and loving Father who is interested and concerned about every single detail of our lives. He personally communicates His Love to each of us, prompting us to say in response, "Lord, I know how much You love me, so no matter what You allow in my life, I will trust You" (Job 13:15).

Susan: "I Gave My Son for You"

One last example of how God communicates His Love:

Susan spent years trying to make God prove to her that He loved her. Growing up, her home life had been, for the most part, largely unstable as her parents were damaged people themselves. She, thus, had difficulty in trusting God for His Love. She believed He loved her in her head, but couldn't seem to see it or feel it in her life experience.

Aching to really know God's Love, Susan walked countless miles at night, waiting for Him to 'talk' to her. She spent one week fasting, praying eight hours a day to get God to communicate His Love to her. She did crazy things, desperate for Him to reveal His Love.

As she tried one thing after another, without 'success,' she grew to feel quite abandoned by God. She begged Him not to leave her or give up on her, as she truly began to fear that He didn't really care about her at all. One night at church, as she leaned against the back wall, an older man stood up to speak and she knew that what he was saying was God talking directly to her. The man said, "God asks you, why do you think that I would ever abandon you? I gave my SON for you. I love you. You are precious to me and I would never ever leave you."

Susan's heart leaped for joy. God was speaking directly to her. She had known all her life that Jesus had died for her, but what overwhelmed her that night was the fact that such *a huge price* had been paid! Since God had invested so much in her, He would never, ever abandon her. After that night, whenever she would begin to doubt God's Love, she would just remind herself, "God loves me so much that He gave His Son for me. And, He must *want* me if He paid so much!"

As time went on, she learned to stop thinking that God didn't love her and replaced it with, "God loves me so much that He gave His SON to die for me. He does love me!"

(If you are interested in learning more about God's personal Love, *The Way of Agape* goes into much greater detail.)

His Love Brings Our Identity & Security

Knowing that God loves us, not only in our head, but also in our everyday life is the only thing that will bring us our true *identity* and *security*. These two things do *not* come from the conditional loves of others, from our physical appearance or from our accomplishments, but only from a personal loving relationship with God.

Jeremiah 31:3 says, "I have loved you with an everlasting Love; therefore with loving-kindness have I drawn you..." And, Hebrews 13:5, "I will *never* leave you or forsake you."

Many people, however, have spent their entire lives trying to find their identity and security in every other conceivable way, rather than in the way that God has designed. They have sought for their families, friends and physical appearance to meet their need for identity and security. And they have looked to their accomplishments, their talents and achievements to meet their need for meaning and purpose. These two needs, however, can *never* be satisfied by other people, things or accomplishments. Momentarily, yes, but long term and inwardly, never. As Philippians 4:19 states, "[Only] My God shall supply *all* your need[s]."

An Example: Prom Queen

Tammy was the most beautiful, most talented and most popular girl in her whole high school. All the girls looked up to her and wanted to be exactly like her. They dressed like her, wore the same clothes as she did and fixed their hair the same exact way.

After Tammy graduated from high school and went on to college, she became a fashion model and won several beauty pageants. When we first met her, she seemed like a very outgoing and very extroverted woman. However, once we really got to know her, we couldn't get over how insecure and self-conscious she was. We asked her if she was a Christian, and she said "yes," but that she had never really felt God's personal Love. Then, she confessed that she had done many of those impressive things in her past simply to cover up for her lack of self-confidence.

As she grew older, she married and had children, but when she gained a few too many pounds and her looks began to fade, she sunk into deep depression. Without her outward beauty, shapely figure and superb talent to hide behind, she lost her identity. Thus, for ten years, she hid and didn't return any phone calls from friends. All of us knew something was terribly wrong, but were helpless to fix it!

Even though Tammy was a Christian, her eyes had always been on the wrong things to bring her that self-esteem and self-worth that she so badly needed. She knew (in her head) that God loved her, but not in her everyday life. Thus, she didn't have the proper foundation upon which to build a true and lasting identity.

We have lost track of Tammy, but the last we heard she had lost some weight and was again trying to make a career for herself, based on her looks and figure. Thus, it seems that her fruitless quest for security and identity still continues. Unfortunately, she will *never* find what she is looking for, until she looks only to Jesus for these things.

God must be the total provision for our security and identity whether we are beautiful, have a gorgeous figure and lots of money, or whether we are unattractive, overweight and poor (Colossians 2:10). When our basic needs for love are being met by God, then whatever we get from our friends, our family or our circumstances is an added blessing. If, however, we are not looking to the Lord to be our security and identity, then, like Tammy, we'll be shaken to the core, if and when these things are ever taken away from us.

We are His "Prized Possessions"

What an incredible identity we do have in Christ. The Bible tells us that we are His prized possessions, His *poema* and His new creations. In Him, we are accepted, complete, alive, forgiven, freed, reconciled, called, chosen, victorious, strong and conquering. Many of us forget these priceless things and we try to add to what God has already done. What for? It's already been done!

It's critical to know that God's Love will never stop coming, no matter what we do or don't do. It will never fail us. And, even when we do blow it badly, God will continue to love us and continue to draw us back to Himself. Just as Psalm 37:23-24 promises: "The steps of a good man are ordered by the Lord; and He delighteth in his way. Though he fall, he shall not be utterly cast down; For the Lord upholdeth him with His hand." (Jeremiah 31:3-4) How patient, longsuffering, forgiving and kind our Father is with us. All He requires of us is to reach up and take a hold of His hand.

One of the reasons we don't fully realize the extent of God's Love, is that we don't really understand that He uses our failures, our mistakes and our errors as a means of drawing us closer to Him. God's view of failure is that He expects it; He forgives it; and then, He uses it. Just as Scripture says, He does work all things together for good to those who love and totally give themselves over to Him (Romans 8:28).

An Example: Mike

God uses our failures and mistakes, not only as a way of bringing us closer to Him, but also as a way of bringing others to Himself. A great example of this is the story of Mike MacIntosh, pastor of Horizon Christian Fellowship in San Diego, California.

As a very young man, Mike tragically became involved in drugs, womanizing and the low life. As a result, he ended up losing his family, becoming critically ill and being confined to the psychiatric ward of a local hospital. At that time, he was told that "he would never amount to anything and would spend the rest of his life in an institution."

The Lord, however, had other plans for this young man. When Mike finally realized his predicament, he cried out to God for mercy and he gave his life to the Lord. God not only heard his cry and took him as His own, He supernaturally healed Mike's mind and body, restored his health and put his family back together. He also began a ministry through Mike that has influenced millions of people. Mike has written several books, been consistently on television and his church has grown into dozens of churches and ministers to thousands upon thousands.

Mike is a wonderful example of God's unconditional Love. Even though God knows we will fail, He is always there to forgive us and weave all that has happened in our lives together to glorify Himself. Truly, that same miracle, that same answer, that same Love is there for all of us. We simply must reach up and grab a hold of it, just like Mike did.

If our identity and security are in God and His unconditional Love, then when we fail, regardless of how badly we have blown it, we still know that we are "a child of the King." Even though we might not feel like it at the time, we know, by faith, that we are loved by the Father, and so by faith, we can pick up the pieces of our lives and begin all over again.

If, however, we are unsure of the fact that God loves us, rather than being able to pick up and start all over again, it becomes almost impossible to accept ourselves as we really are, and this is where the "game playing" begins. We either justify our failures and make excuses for them or we try to hide and cover them up. Even if we do the latter successfully, the memory of those failures still lingers in our minds and it becomes the motivation to constantly prove ourselves, not only to others, but to ourselves. It's a vicious circle that we will never emerge from!

This is why it's essential to be so secure in God's Love, that when failures occur in our lives (and they will because we are human), we'll know that God will use them as a way of binding us even closer to Him. Remember Drew's, Sandy's and Mike's stories. The end result of seeing God use our mistakes "for good" is that we'll realize His Love for us to an even greater degree than we did before. God's unconditional forgiveness in our lives only proves that He loves us all the more.

That inner identity and security that we are all looking for can only come from knowing that God loves us personally.

Do You Know That God Loves You?

Most Christians, if you asked them, would tell you in all honesty, that they really don't know that God loves them. They know about Him and they know His Word, but they really don't know His Love in a daily, personal way. They really don't have that daily, living experience of Him. Now, the reason it's so important to personally know God's Love, is because when we see His handprint of Love in every aspect of our lives, we'll never fear what He might allow into our lives. We'll know that everything He allows is by His permission and will ultimately be used for His purposes in our lives.

Knowing God loves us is the only thing that will give us hope for the future. Hope that leads to faith and the ability to trust Him in everything, regardless of what is going on. God's Love is what will help us endure, persevere and hang on through the trials, through the testings and through the chastenings.

Hope in God's Love is what will give us the faith to look beyond the near term, beyond the current situation and beyond the horrendous problems, and look to Him for our final victory. If we know without a doubt that we are loved by the Father, then there is always hope for the future!

Questions from Chapter Two

1) Why is it so important to personally know that God loves us? Share your own thoughts.

2) Can you describe an incident in your life where you felt God's unconditional Love? Why is it easier to make good decisions when you are confident of His Love?

3) How does God communicate His Love? Why can't we always count on our circumstances to show us His Love?

4) Describe how knowing God loves us gives us our security and identity? What is your identity and security built upon? Be honest...

5) God's Love is always there. What do we do to sabotage our confidence in His Love? How can we restore our confidence? (See "Supplemental Study," page 165 and 162 for a *visual picture* of this.)

* If you want the suggested answers to these questions, they are available on our website **www.kingshighway.org**, under the *Plain and Simple Series*, or you can write us at the address on the back of this book, or call us.

How I Feel About Myself

Answer these questions as quickly as you can. Take them in the order they appear. Don't change any of your answers, your first impression is the right one.

1) I think about my appearance...
   - constantly.
   - regularly.
   - when it is called to my attention.
   - rarely.
   - never (even when looking in a mirror).

2) The money I spend on clothes and my appearance is...
   - ridiculous.
   - too much.
   - about right.
   - not enough.

3) I dress the way I do for church on Sundays primarily because...
   - I feel most comfortable this way.
     it is what others expect.
   - I don't want to be noticed or to stick out.
   - I want others to notice me.
   - I think God would be pleased.
   - I was taught by my parents to dress this way.
   - (Fill in another reason...)

4) Quite honestly, I...
   - judge people on the basis of their appearance.
   - don't let appearance affect how I think of people.

- Let appearance affect the way I judge people, and rightly so.
- try not to be affected by people's appearance but can't help it.

5) I dress the way I do at work or at school because...

- I feel most comfortable that way.
- It's what others expect.
- I don't want to be noticed or stick out.
- I want others to notice me.
- I think God would be pleased.
- I was taught by my parents to dress this way.
- I would lose my job or be kicked out of school if I dressed otherwise.
- (Fill in another reason...)

6) List the above seven reasons for dressing the way one does, from *best* (#1) to *worst* (#7).

7) Most people in our society...
- are hung up on appearance.
- don't care enough about their appearance.
- have a good perspective on the importance of appearance.
- (Fill in another viewpoint...)

8) If I could change one thing about my appearance, it would be...

9) The reason I would change my appearance is that...
- I would impress others more favorably.
- I would be able to put my concerns about my appearance behind me.

- I would be better in sports.
- I would feel better physically.
- I would be more attractive to the opposite sex.
- (Fill in another reason...)

10) Please rate the following three items as to whether you think they matter very much to God (A), matter very little to God (B), matter to God if they matter to us (C) or, really don't matter at all to God (D).
    - How I dress_____
    - Whether I am overweight or underweight__
    - Whether I shower, shave, keep my hair combed or cut regularly_____

11) A Christian in our society... (mark which answer best describes your feelings)
    - should have about the same ideas as others in our culture about appearance. In other words, there is little wrong with how our society judges appearances.
    - should be distinctly different from most of our society in the way he thinks about appearance. In other words, our society should not judge so much by appearance.

12) When I am dressed distinctly different from others in a social situation, I feel...
    - pleased.
    - embarrassed and conspicuous.
    - comfortable.
    - (Fill in another viewpoint...)

Knowing God Loves me
(The following Scriptures are paraphrased)

Herein is Love, not that we loved God, but that He loved us and sent His Son to be the propitiation [substitute offering] for our sins (1 John 4:10).

He bowed the heavens also, and came down (Psalm 18:9).

He sent from above, He took me, He drew me out of many waters (Psalm 18:16).

The Lord appeared unto me saying, `Yea, I have loved thee with an everlasting Love' (Jeremiah 31:3).

I have engraved thee upon the palms of my hand (Isaiah 49:16).

I will never leave thee or forsake thee (Hebrews 13:5).

For the mountains shall depart and the hills be removed; but my Lovingkindness [chesed] shall not depart from thee, neither shall my covenant of peace [rest] be removed, saith the Lord that hath mercy on thee (Isaiah 54:10).

As the heaven is high above the earth, so great is His Mercy [lovingkindness] towards them that fear Him (Psalm 103:11).

Many are the afflictions of the righteous. But the Lord delivers them out of them all. He keepeth all his bones; not a one of them is broken (Psalm 34:19-20).

When you pass through the waters [trouble] I will be with you; and through the rivers, they won't overflow you; when you walk through the fire, you won't be burned; neither shall the flame kindle upon thee. For I am the Lord...You are precious in My sight and I love you (Isaiah 43:2-4).

God commendeth His Love toward us in that, while we were yet sinners, Christ died for us (Romans 5:8).

For God so loved the world, that He gave His only begotten Son (John 3:16).

Greater Love hath no man than this, that a man lay down his life for his friends (John 15:13).

Behold, what manner of Love the Father hath bestowed upon us, that we should be called the sons of God (1 John 3:1).

...having loved His own which were in the world, He loved them unto the end (John 13:1).

What shall separate us from the Love of Christ? Shall tribulation, or distress, or persecution, or famine, or nakedness, or peril, or sword?...I am persuaded that neither death, nor life, nor angels, nor principalities, nor powers, nor things present, nor things to come, nor height, nor depth, nor any other creature shall be able to separate us from the Love of God which is in Christ Jesus, our Lord (Romans 8:35, 38-39).

Who I Am in Christ

The Word of God states that if I am *born again* I am:

Reconciled to God (2 Corinthians 5:18);

A son of God (1 John 3:1);

A new creature (2 Corinthians 5:17);

Called of God (2 Timothy 1:9);

Chosen (1 Thessalonians 1:4; Ephesians 1:4; 1 Peter 2:9);

The temple of the Holy Spirit (1 Corinthians 6:19);

Holy and without blame before Him in Love (Ephesians 1:4);

A partaker of His divine nature (2 Peter 1:4);

In Christ Jesus by His doing (1 Corinthians 1:30);

Accepted in the Beloved (Ephesians 1:6);

Beloved of God (Colossians 3:12; Romans 1:7; 1 Thessalonians 1:4);

Complete in Him (Colossians 2:10);

Alive with Christ (Ephesians 2:5);

The apple of my Father's eye (Deut. 32:10; Psalm 17:8);

Forgiven of all my sins and washed in His Blood (Ephesians 1:7; Hebrews 9:14; Colossians 1:14; 1 John 1:9; 2:12);

Healed by the stripes of JESUS (1 Peter 2:24; Isaiah 53:5);

Delivered from the power of darkness and translated into God's kingdom (Colossians 1:13);

Set free (John 8:31-33);

Kept by God and the evil one does not touch me (1 John 5:18);

Free from condemnation (Romans 8:1);

Dead to sin (Romans 6:2, 11; 1 Peter 2:24);

God's workmanship created in Christ Jesus for good works (Ephesians 2:10);

Being changed into His Image (2 Corinthians 3:18; Philippians 1:6);

Victorious (Revelation 21:7);

Strong in the Lord (Ephesians 6:10);

More than a conqueror (Romans 8:37);

The righteousness of God in Him (2 Corinthians 5:21);

The light of the world (Matthew 5:14);

An ambassador for Christ (2 Corinthians 5:20);

The salt of the earth (Matthew 5:13);

Sealed with the Holy Spirit of promise (Ephesians 1: 13);

Joint heirs with Christ (Romans 8:17);

Raised up with Christ (Ephesians 2:6);

Partakers of His inheritance (Colossians 1:12);

Established to the end (1 Corinthians 1:8);

Firmly rooted, built up, established in the faith and abounding with thanksgiving (Colossians 2:7);

In this world as He is (1 John 4:17).

Chapter Three
What is Our Responsibility?

Keep My Commandments

Now that we understand that God loves us with an unending, never failing and forgiving Love, what is our own responsibility in living His Life? What must "we" do in order to move forward in our walk with Him? What does God want from us?

The Bible says that the most important thing that God wants from us, is for us *to learn to love Him*. Remember, Deuteronomy 30:20 which says, "That you might love the Lord thy God...obey His voice, and...cleave unto Him: for He is your Life." By loving Him, obeying Him and cleaving unto Him we will be responding to His Love in the way that He desires. In other words, once we know that He loves us, our responsibility is to love Him in return. As the Bible states, "We love Him, because He first loved us." (1 John 4:19)

Okay. What exactly does it mean to love Him? Are we talking about an emotional love here where we experience a warm tingling feeling when we sing about Him? Is this loving Him? Does loving Him mean knowing Scriptures backwards and forwards? Are we loving Him when we attend church regularly or when we raise our hands in worship? What exactly does loving God really mean?

John 14:15 says that, "If you love Me, [then] keep My commandments." (1 John 5:3; John 14:21) Well, that sounds great, but which commandments does He mean? There are hundreds of them! Well, Galatians 5:14, Matthew 22:40 and Romans 13:10 all tell us, that the whole Bible is really summed up in only *two* commandments. And they are:

"Thou shalt love (*agapao*) the Lord thy God with all thy heart, with all thy soul, and with all thy mind. This is the first and great commandment. And the second is like unto it, Thou shalt love (*agapao*) thy neighbor as thyself." (Matthew 22:37-39)

Also Deut. 6

These two commandments are inseparable and must go in the order that they were given. In other words, we *can't* learn to love others as ourselves until we have *first* learned to love God with all our heart, mind and soul. We must first love God— become that open and cleansed vessel—then *He* can love others *through us*.

One of the reasons why the Christian body is having such a hard time trying to live the Christian life, is because it has mixed up these two commandments. In other words, most of us have been out there trying to love others, *before* we have any idea of what it really means to love God with all our heart, mind and soul.

Agapao Defined

The Greek word for "love" used in both of the great commandments is the verb *agapao*. To *agapao* something means *to totally give ourselves over to it,* to be completely consumed with it, or entirely committed to it. What we *agapao* is what we put first in our lives. All our intentions and abilities are focused and consumed with this one thing. In other words, to *agapao* something means to so bind ourselves with something that we almost become "one" with it.

The confusing part is that this commitment love (*agapao*) can either be to God, to man or to things of the world. Read the following Scriptures and see what people in the Bible "totally gave themselves over to." The Greek word in each of these Scriptures is *agapao*:

John 3:19, "men loved *darkness* rather than light, because their deeds were evil."

John 12:43, "For they loved *the praise of men* more than the praise of God."

Luke 11:43, "Woe unto you, Pharisees! for ye love *the uppermost seats* in the synagogues."

2 Timothy 4:10, "For Demas hath forsaken me, having loved *this present world.*"

1 John 2:15, "Love not *the world*, neither the things that are in the world."

And lastly, Luke 6:32, "for sinners also love *those that love them.*"

Some current examples of things that we *agapao* are careers, money, ungodly relationships, pleasure, *self*, etc.

Do You Love God?

If I asked you, "Do you love [*agapao*] God?", most of you would probably automatically say, "Yes, of course I do!"

But if you are really honest with yourself, how often do you *totally give yourself over to Him* and seek to put His Will and His Desires above your own? How often are you consumed with what He desires for your life and not what you want out of life? *Can you honestly say that you desire His Will above your own happiness?* Most of the world is seeking happiness and contentment as their ultimate goal. Is that your goal? Or is it to set yourself aside and live Life as God designed?

An Example: "Not my will, but Thine"

Amy was in Bible College, surrounded by 'eligible men'. Many of them were her good friends and they were bright and fun, and claimed Jesus as their Savior. All her teenage years, Amy had held off from dating, and now she decided it was time that she find a husband. As she watched many of her friends pairing off, however, she felt God saying to her heart, "Do you want what *you* want, or do you want *I* want?"

More than anything else, she wanted to be married. She wanted a husband and children and a home with a front porch and oak trees and a little garden. Her own parents had been divorced when she was seven, so she longed for a family of her own.

After a day or two of wrestling with this decision, Amy told God that she would trust His will, in spite of her feelings. She set her own will and desires aside and said, "Okay Lord, I want what you want. I know You know what is best for me. And, even if I never get married, that's okay. I want Your will and not my own."

This decision was one of the hardest she had ever made. However, as soon as she had put her will aside and decided to choose God's, she felt *free*. She no longer had to look at every man and ask, "I wonder if that's him." She didn't have to waste her time and her heart on a series of dead-end relationships. She didn't have to worry about it. She knew that God would take care of everything.

After college, God moved Amy to a little community in Northern Idaho to help start a youth ministry. She quickly became close to her church family and developed true, sincere relationships. She would often tell her pastor, "I might never be married," and he would just smile and say, "Oh yes you will."

One night when praising God, Amy realized how close she had become to Jesus, and how she had learned to lean on Him and enjoy just having Him as her partner in life. She poured her heart out to Him and said she still would very much like a husband, but expressed her commitment to still only marry if it was *His* desire.

Two days later, God showed Amy the man she was to marry, a friend named Drew (who we met last chapter in the example, "Beauty for Ashes"). Now, he was the *last* person in the entire world that she would have expected, and she said to God, "What? Not him! That's crazy!" However, she added, "But, I know if that's what You want, it will be *good*." And, she had confidence in that.

After that, Amy learned to *really* depend on God. It was a difficult and an emotional time, with many questions, but God was faithful. Daily, He revealed to her, through a host of hard circumstances, the true quality of this man—how much he loved and truly followed Jesus, his complete trust in God and his honest, unselfish love towards her. Ultimately, she grew to see how this friend complemented her personality, even better than she could have ever dared to hope. Over the next one and a half years, they became the best of friends, fell in love and, eventually, were married.

Amy had given *her* will over to God, and God performed *His* perfect will in her life.

This is an example of real Christianity.

Real Meaning of Loving God

Thus, to love God is not an emotional feeling. To love God the way He designed means to relinquish and yield ourselves over to Him (all our thoughts, emotions, and desires that are contrary to His), so that His Life can come forth from our hearts. (See page 162 in "Supplemental Study" for a *visual picture* of how this works.)

2 Corinthians - transformed into likeness

2 Corinthians 4:10-11 says it best, "Always bearing about in the body the dying of the Lord Jesus, that the life also of Jesus might be made manifest in our body. For we who live are always delivered unto death for Jesus' sake, [so] that the life also of Jesus might be made manifest in our mortal flesh."

Isaiah 15

In other words, to love God (*agapao*) simply means to become a cleansed and open vessel so Jesus' Life can be shown forth through us!

Romans 12:1

Because of our ignorance as to what loving God really means, we often get our "feeling" love confused and mixed up with this "commitment" love (*agapao*). And because most of us have great emotional love for God, we think we are loving Him in the way that He desires when, in fact, we're not even close. Loving God really has nothing to do with our "feelings," but simply the *willingness* to give everything to God. And that, of course, is our constant choice!

An Example: "Not Your Will, but mine!"

In contrast to Amy's story, here's a story that seems all-too-common these days...

With great enthusiasm, Melissa turned her life over to Christ. She gave up smoking, sex, drugs and partying, and could be found in the church every time it opened its doors. For the first few months, things went perfectly. She felt close to God, and knew that He had good things planned for her. At times, she could feel His presence and His Love, which she so desperately needed. Soon, however, she became burdened with rules and regulations and the realization of how hard it was to "be good." On several occasions she would slip into her old ways, and, afterwards, would be filled with intense guilt. On the surface, she was still cheerful, friendly Melissa. She continued to go to church and bring her friends, but she began to do it because she felt she was "supposed to," not because she wanted to. Inside, she felt suffocated, pressured and miserable. This was not the freedom and peace and abundant life that she had expected!

After a year she fell back into her old lifestyle. It was just easier, and besides, she then didn't have to feel badly about herself. She finally stopped going to church altogether and began to hang out with her old friends.

When she was fifteen, Melissa found out she was pregnant. She knew she was too young to raise a child, but she longed to be a mother. When she lost the baby, she fell into a deep depression and thoughts of suicide constantly filled her mind.

During this time, many people began praying intensely for Melissa. Over time, she began to attend church again. Finally, at a huge youth convention in Seattle, Melissa, once again, felt the power of God's Love cover her and cleanse her. It wasn't the big emotional rush she had felt when she first gave her life to Christ, but she knew God had touched her. The joy she originally had known in God returned, and she came home refreshed and renewed.

As time went on, however, the fire in her heart again slowly died. This time, it stemmed from one single decision. There was an old friend with whom she was "in love." God had made it very clear to her, over and over again, that she needed to separate herself from him. He was not a believer and a very bad influence. But, by this time, her emotions had totally consumed her and she just couldn't. Her response to the Lord was, "I want *my* will, Lord, not *Your's*."

Time will only tell how far she has to fall and how battered she has to get, before she realizes that *there really is no other choice*, but to "choose Life" and live it as God desires.

It's impossible to *strattle the fence*—one day live for God and the next, for self—and expect to live a blessed and abundant Life. It doesn't work that way! We will end up getting ripped up the middle. We must commit to faithfully (as best we can) making *The Choice* to, moment by moment, let Christ live His Life out through us.

The Practical Application of Loving God

Thus, loving God simply means surrendering the things in our lives that are "not of faith" and becoming an open and cleansed vessel so that His Life can flow from our hearts out into our lives. The only way this is possible, however, is by knowing exactly *how* to give our sin and self over to the Lord. Our sin and self are the two things that continually stand in the way of our being cleansed vessels.

All of us talk about giving things to God, but most of the time we end up taking those things back three minutes later. The question is, "How do we give things that are 'not of faith' to God and leave them there?"

The steps we are about to learn are not just steps that I have made up or gotten from some self-help book. They are the actual steps that the priests of Solomon's Temple in the Old Testament went through in order to deal with their sin and be reconciled with God. I believe God has laid these steps out in Scripture so that we might know "how" to deal with our sin and self and be reconciled to God.

Going through these cleansing steps every time we are confronted with a hurtful remark, a painful situation, pride, fear, doubt, anxiety, bitterness, resentment (whatever is not of faith or whatever blocks His Love in our heart), is the only way we can stay open vessels so that God's Life can flow from our hearts out into our souls.

The Four Essential Steps:

1) *Recognize, acknowledge and experience* the negative thoughts and emotions that have just occurred. Don't vent these feelings, and

certainly, don't push them down. Get alone with
God and experience your emotions. Name how
you are feeling. Ask Him to expose the real *root
cause* of your ungodly thoughts and feelings.

2) *Confess and repent* of any negative thoughts and
    feelings that are "not of faith" or that you have
    held onto for awhile. Choose to "turn around"
    from following what these things are telling you
    to do and choose instead, to follow what God
    is saying. Also, *unconditionally forgive anyone
    else* involved. God then, will forgive your sins.

3) *Give over to God* all that He has shown you,
    not only the conscious negative thoughts and
    emotions, but also their "root" causes. (See
    page 167-168 in "Supplemental Study" on
    hidden chambers.) He, then, will purge your sin
    and reconcile you to Himself.

4) *Read God's Word*. Be sure to replace any lies
    in your thinking with His Truth (His Word).
    God will then cleanse and heal your soul
    with the "washing of the water of the Word"
    (Ephesians 5:26).

    At this point, by faith (whether you feel like it
or not), God will have emptied you of self-life and
filled you back up with His Life. Because you have
loved Him, He now can enable you to go on and love
others.

    Loving God (totally giving ourselves over to
Him in this way) is the KEY to letting Christ live
His Life out through us and the KEY to the abundant

Life. Again, it's His Life, but always our choice to implement it. (We have just completed another *Plain and Simple* little book called *The Key* which describes all of these steps in much greater detail.) It's easy to say, "Oh, just give it to God. But, *how* do we do this on a moment-by-moment basis?

An Example: Danny's Story

Here's a perfect example of how these steps work in real life.

It was a beautiful summer morning and the air was still and quiet—a perfect morning to go for a horseback ride. Danny loved any excuse to ride and today his cousin was in town. They packed up their gear and the two of them, plus Danny's older brother, saddled up and rode off into the mountains.

They rode all day long and had a grand time. On their way back down the hill, they decided to gallop. The sun was going down so the shadows were long and dark. Neither Danny nor his horse saw the log laying in the middle of the trail and before they knew it, the horse had tripped, fallen on him and mangled his leg from his groin to his upper thigh.

When the paramedics arrived, there was the fear that Danny might not even make it, because he had lost so much blood. He ended up in the hospital for nearly two months.

Because of the seriousness of his injuries, Danny could not attend school for several months. His mom tried to help him with some of his lessons at home, but still the majority of his work had to be made up at a later date. Miraculously, when the report cards were sent out, he received all A's and B's except two C's in classes where he was unable to catch up.

However, when his dad saw his report card, rather than being thrilled and focusing on the A's and B's, he became angry and thoughtlessly said, "You're never going to amount to anything." Danny was crushed beyond words. Slowly, he limped back to his room and waited for his mom to come home. His mom was his real friend and he could trust her. When she returned and Danny told her what had happened, she held him and said, "Danny, only Jesus loves us perfectly. Let's take that hurt (what your dad said to you) to Jesus." Together, they did just that. They went through the above steps and the next day, Danny said that the hurt was really gone and that he was fine. He even said he was going to keep on loving his dad, no matter what.

The mom plans to confront the dad, in God's timing and way, for his unwise and unloving remark.

This is a real-life example of how a young Christian can make *The Choice* to stay an open and cleansed vessel so that God's Life could continue to flow, in spite of the real hurt and emotions he felt.

This way of loving explains how God expects us to love (*to totally give ourselves over to*) the untrustworthy, the despicable and even, our enemies (Luke 6:27). Humanely speaking, unconditionally loving them, of course, is impossible! However, as we totally give ourselves over to God, He then gives us His Love for them. So, even though a person might be completely unlovable to us, God still loves them, and, all He needs from us is openness so that He might pour His Love for them *through* us.

Complete Surrender of Self

Thus, to love God in the way that He designed is *not* an emotional feeling; it's not raising our hands in church or knowing Scriptures backwards and forwards. To love God the way He desires means *to totally give our self over to Him.* "Self," as we said before, is all our own thoughts, emotions and desires that are contrary to God's or that are not of faith. God wants us to continually relinquish ourselves to Him and allow His Life to come forth, just like Danny did.

John 12:24 explains: "Except a corn of wheat fall into the ground and die, it abideth alone [no fruit]: but if it die, it bringeth forth much fruit [God's Love]."

The Choice to do this, moment by moment, is what makes us a *real* Christian, because then it's God's Life that comes forth and not our own.

Yielding ourselves to God does not mean surrendering who we really are and becoming some sort of a mindless robot. No, relinquishing ourselves simply means setting aside all our thoughts, emotions and desires that are not of faith and becoming a cleansed and open vessel (or channel). Then, God's

Life from our hearts can fill our souls and freely flow through us to others. It's still our own personality, our own talents and our own creativity, but it's now God's Life through us. This is the point at which we can say Jesus is not just *in* my life, but as Deuteronomy 30:20 tells us; He *is* my very life itself!

As Paul reiterates in Philippians 1:21, "For me to live is Christ..."

Meaning and Purpose of our Lives

Learning to love God and others is really the meaning and purpose of our lives as Christians. We've been called for two primary reasons: *To learn to love Him, and then to learn to love others.* We haven't been called just to be content within ourselves and satisfied with our own lives, but to be channels of His Love and Life, not only experiencing it for ourselves, but also passing it along to others.

1 Timothy 1:5 confirms that *Agape* is the goal of our instruction and the fulfillment of all of God's Word in us! In other words, the whole Bible is summed up in our personally knowing and passing on God's Love (Romans 13:10; Matthew 22:40).

God declares in 1 Corinthians 13 that without His Love and His Life flowing through us, all the intellectual knowledge in the world, all the wisdom and understanding in the world and all the faith in the world will profit us nothing. Without His Love, He says, we will be empty, lonely and without meaning or purpose to our lives. Without His Love, God says, "We are nothing" (1 Corinthians 13:3).

An Example: Dutch

A few years ago, Dutch, a Viet Nam veteran, came into our ministry offices looking for Chuck and me. This dear man had lost an arm, a hand, an ear and an eye in the war, and had many other physical disabilities besides. When he saw us, he burst into tears, grabbed the two of us and began to tell us his incredible story:

He had been a Christian for over 18 years, but had struggled for most of those years trying to find meaning and purpose for his life. Understandably, he had suffered severe marital and relationship problems, financial problems, as well as many other serious physical problems. He told us how he had become a part of several church outreaches, trying to find personal fulfillment. But, he said, *"something was always missing."*

Then someone handed him *The Way of Agape* book on loving the way God designed; he said his life changed forever. Through that little book, Dutch learned that God's purpose in choosing him was to conform him into His image of Love, so that Love could flow *through him* to others. Dutch told us how God had begun to work this message of Love into his life and how he was beginning to see himself genuinely change from the inside out. He said he had finally found what his real meaning and purpose was as a Christian: *to be a cleansed vessel so that God can love His Love through him.* Dutch then went on to say, *"The neat part is, that it doesn't matter what that vessel looks like. The important thing is that God's Love flows through it."*

Love is the whole reason God created us in the first place, and if we don't learn to love and be loved in the way He intends, we truly will have wasted our lives and missed the whole point of our being called.

"Priceless, Yet Worthless, Possessions"

Many people, after working their entire lives to reach their own personal goals (to be happy, to have their own business, to have financial independence, etc.), realize too late that their meaning and purpose does *not* come from material things, careers, wealth, etc. Here's another perfect example:

Many years ago, there was a newspaper article that told the story of a very famous and wealthy man. He was the founder of a huge aero space firm. Throughout his life he thought God, love, family and children were just a nuisance and a deterrent to what success was all about. He determined to amass a fortune for himself and to make his name known worldwide. He did both. But in the process, he lost all of his personal love-relationships and, in the end, when he was too old to work anymore and his eyesight was nearly gone, he sat night after night, alone in his huge, empty mansion, filled with priceless—yet worthless—possessions. This wealthy man had missed out on the whole reason he was created—to love and to be loved.

Edgar Jackson wrote an excellent book called *Understanding Loneliness*. In it, he shares how psychologists have now exchanged the word "identity" for the word *love*. Love, they say, is our true identity.

Without love we are lost, regardless of how much money, power, prestige and education we amass. Love must be the supreme and central issue of our lives, otherwise we will die psychologically, socially, spiritually and even physically.

He Is Our Life

This complete surrender of our selves to God is the union and the oneness that He desires for every one of us: *One heart, one will and one life.* He wants us to become so "at one" with Him, that what others see and hear through us is *His* Love, *His* Wisdom and *His* Power. In other words, it's His Life and His character coming forth from us and not our own. This is what it means to be a *real* Christian. (Again, see *visual picture* of this in "Supplemental Study" on page 162.)

In John 21:15-17, Peter is asked three times by Jesus, "Do you love Me?" The first two times Jesus uses the word, *agapao*, "are you able to totally give yourself over to me?" "Will you surrender yourself to Me?" "Will you become *one* with Me?" Peter, however, could only answer back, "Lord I have friendship love (*phileo*) for you." (At least Peter was being honest.) The final time Jesus asks Peter, "Do you love Me?" Jesus comes down to Peter's level and uses the word *phileo*. "Peter, do you at least have friendship love for Me?" Peter was grieved because he knew that Jesus knew, at that particular time, he was not able to totally relinquish himself to Him (*agapao*).

Jesus is asking us the very same questions: "Do you love (*agapao*) Me? Will you totally give yourself over to Me? Will you lay down your will and your life so I can live My Life out through you? Will you become One with Me? Will you *Choose Life*?"

What is your answer?

Again, "Strait is the gate, and narrow is the way, which leadeth unto life, and few there be that find it" (Matthew 7:14).

Will you be one who does?

Questions From Chapter Three

1) In the past, what did you believe *loving God* meant? What have you learned that it really means? Why is it so important to know this?

2) What is **The Choice** that Christians are constantly faced with?

3) If we really can't fix or repair our self life, what are we to do with it?

4) Do you love Jesus enough to allow His Life to be poured *through* you? What if He asks you to do something you don't want to do? Describe your feelings on this.

5) Write out in your own words the steps to loving God. Do you have to "feel" like doing these steps when you totally give yourself over to God?

6) What is it that gives our lives *meaning* and *purpose*? What have you been relying upon to fulfill these needs? Be honest.

* If you want the suggested answers to these questions, they are available on our website **www.kingshighway.org**, under the *Plain and Simple Series*, or you can write us at the address on the back of the book, or call us.

How We Love (*agapao*) God

1) *Recognize, acknowledge and experience the negative thoughts and emotions that have just occurred* (2 Corinthians 10:5).
   A. Don't vent these or push them down, get alone with God.
   B. Try to describe to God how you are feeling and what you are thinking.
   Then, you will know exactly what to give God in the next few steps.
   C. Ask Him to expose any *root causes* for your ungodly thoughts, emotions or actions (Prov. 20:27; Job 12:22; 1 Cor. 4:5).

2) *Confess your sin and self, repent of it and unconditionally forgive anyone else involved* (Prov. 1:23; 28:13; James 4:8-10; 1 John 1:9; Col. 3:13; Is. 1:16).
   A. Confess everything that God shows you is "not of faith" and choose to turn around (repent of it). Choose to follow what God is telling you to do. Just asking God to forgive you is not enough, you must first confess that you have sinned, and then repent of it. This is your own responsibility.
   B. Unconditionally forgive anyone who has wronged you (Matt. 6:14-15; 18-35; Col. 3:13). You have asked God's forgiveness for your sins; now you must forgive others of theirs.
   C. Know that God has forgiven you (1 John 1: 9; Matt. 6:14; Ps. 32:5).

3) ***Give over to God all that He has shown you***
(even the "justified" things) (Col. 3:5, 8; 1 Peter
5:7-8a; Gal. 5:24-26; Rom. 6:11-13).
   A. Ask God to get rid of these things for you
   (Ps. 103:12; Is. 6:1-7).
   B. By faith, believe that He has done so.
   C. Ask Him to change your feelings to match
   your "faith choice" (1 Jn. 3:21-24).

4) ***Get into the Word and replace the lies with the
truth*** (Luke 11:24-26; Eph. 5:26; John 15:3; 17:
17; Ps. 19:7-8).
   A. God will then heal your soul with the
   "washing of water by the Word" (Ps. 18; 51:
   7; 107:20; 119:9; Phil. 3:13).
   B. Only God's Word can totally restore you.
   C. At this point, by faith, you have been
   washed, renewed and cleansed.

Chapter Four
Passing Christ's Life Along

The Church's Lack of Love

As we look around—at our churches, our families and our friends—we see many who are dying from a lack of love. These Christians are not only unable to experience God's Love for themselves, but also unable to love others as God designed. Thus, they have resorted to living the Christian life in their own power and strength and have thrown themselves into *other* Christian "things"—such as, the gifts and outpouring of the Spirit, healing ministries, doctrinal debates, faith movements and other various evangelical outreaches, etc. (Now, it's not that any of these things are bad in themselves, but without God's Love alongside, the Bible says they will be meaningless and empty). As a result, these believers have lost the true meaning of their lives, which as we said, is being loved and loving as God designed. Revelation 2:4 very appropriately speaks to these kinds of Christians and says, "You have left (or *covered up*) your first love."

God's Love is the glue that binds us together and tragically it's missing in many of our lives. It's only Jesus' Love through us—in our actions—that will bring our families and our friends and neighbors to the feet of Jesus. *God is Love and the only way these people will ever know that we are, indeed, Christians is by the Love that they see and feel through us.*

A precious friend said to me yesterday, "I thought Christianity was all about *love and acceptance*." This young woman was in the process of becoming a Christian, but the church she has chosen to attend is giving her a very hard time because she is in the middle of a divorce. They have, unfortunately, put the cart before the horse and are judging her *even before* she comes to Christ. Where is the Love? Where are the *real* Christians?

Another example: Megan was about to marry the "love of her life." Everything had already been purchased for the wedding, including the bridesmaids' outfits, the honeymoon spot and their furnished dream home. Megan had given up her job and literally *everything* to move to the city where her fiancé worked.

Tragically, when her engagement was broken off just two months before the wedding, on top of feeling rejected and unloved, Megan had to again move. She had to find another job and endure the humiliation of seeking financial support from her family. Megan was completely broken and devastated by the whole experience. As she explained, "it was like going from almost *perfect happiness* to *total emptiness and loss*".

In her new location, she made friends quickly and became quite close to a few Christian women. However, soon Megan heard that some of the women were gossiping about her. This made her feel even more unloved and rejected.

What she needed was the loving arms of Christian brothers and sisters who would encourage her back to emotional stability. What she received, however, was judgment and criticism. She heart-breakingly said, "My non-Christian friends in my old city were much more loyal and caring than some of my new Christian friends. Why?"

Something Is Very Wrong!

Sadly, both of these young women have totally been turned off by the behavior and attitude of the Christian body towards them. Something is very wrong! Aren't we supposed to be a "hospital" where the stronger ones are to care for the weaker? Aren't we supposed to continually forgive each other, exhort each other and love each other? We often jokingly say, "Oh yea, Christians are the only ones who form their own firing squads in circles." We laugh about that and kid each other, but how tragic it is that no one seems to care enough to stop it.

God's Love doesn't just fall out of heaven. His Love comes through us. *We* are His arms and legs. We are extensions of His Love and His Life to one another. Remember the wonderful story of the German pastor imprisoned by the sadistic guard? That pastor had every right to hate his tormentor and yet, because he loved God, he made ***The Choice*** to be an open vessel of God's Love to that guard. As you remember, God's Love finally broke through and the guard admitted that he saw the face of Jesus in that humble pastor.

This is *real* Christianity! This is God's will and this is the kind of Life that will bring others to Jesus.

Larry Crabb, in his book *Inside Out*, shares that Christians can spend years reading the Bible and developing a real love for the truth; but, if they come away without knowing God in a deeper and more real way and without His Love for people, then they will have wasted their time. The whole purpose of Bible study is to make us more loving, not more scholarly.

David Needham in his book *Birthright* confirms this same thought: "...the big task is not the finding of the truth, but the living of it!" And this is so true. Many of us know the truth in our heads, but very few of us are walking it out in our lives.

Extensions of His Love

If so many people are Spirit filled, as they claim to be today, then why don't our churches, our homes, our marriages and our relationships reflect this? *How can we be "Spirit filled" and not love filled? Aren't they the same thing?*

Love, to me, is simply the measure by which we can tell how "Spirit filled" a person is.

God's Love and Life are passed on through *us*. We are His "arms and legs" in this world. *We are extensions of His Love*. All He requires of us is a cleansed life. Now, being a vessel of God's Love doesn't really sound too complicated? Why, then, are there not more examples of this in the Christian body? If Jesus is *in us* and we have His Love in our hearts, why then, are we having such a difficult time loving others as He designed?

The answer is, we don't know *how* to make ***The Choice*** to let Christ live His Life out through us. We don't know how to *choose Life!* We don't know how to set ourselves aside and love God, so that He then can love others through us.

1 Peter 1:22 sums up what loving God means, but it also instructs us as to *what we are to do now*: "Seeing ye have purified your souls in obeying the truth through the Spirit unto unfeigned Love of the brethren, [now] *see that ye love [agapao] one another with* [from] *a pure heart fervently."*

Now, it's true that until we learn to really love God, there's no way we can genuinely love others as ourselves. In other words, it's impossible to totally give ourselves over to another, until we have *first* totally given ourselves over to God. Only God can make loving others possible. Once we have loved Him, however, we must go on and be those open channels of His Love to others. (For a *visual picture* of this, see page 162 in "Supplemental Study.")

As 1 John 4:21 admonishes us, "And this commandment have we from Him, that he who loveth God [must also] love his brother."

An Example: Walter's Story

A young teenage girl named Terri worked in a backwoods steak house. One evening, she watched as a short bearded man walked in and sat up at the bar.

She first noticed his eyes, because they were bright blue, but hard and angry. While she worked back and forth, she found out that his name was Walter, and he found out that she was going to Bible College to become a missionary.

"Well, I don't believe in God," Walter said.

Rather than arguing with him, Terri simply asked him, "Why?" As he sat there, he told her that a large number of people in his family had died suddenly, and that he had never forgiven God for it and had decided that either God didn't really love him, or that He was not real.

Feeling compassion for this dusty, angry man, Terri asked Walter if he'd ever talked to God about it. Had he been honest with God and told Him he was angry with Him? God could take it, she grinned.

After talking some more, Terri asked Walter if she could pray for him, and there in the bar, with the bartender and all the other customers watching, she put her arm across Walter's shoulders and spoke to God on his behalf. Immediately after that, she escaped to the back of the restaurant, where the dumpsters were, and she wept and wept for Walter and asked God to please show the man that He loved him.

What she didn't realize is that God had already showed Walter how much He loved him, by sending her to pray with him. He was just another dusty logger who had come in for a steak. There was no reason in the world why Terri should have had a heart for him, and yet, God used Terri, because she was available to communicate His Love to Walter.

Six months later, Walter came back in to visit Terri. When he first walked in, she immediately noticed his eyes because this time they were bright blue and full of light and joy. He had finally chosen to leave all his questions and doubt at the Cross, and accept Christ into his heart, and "wow!" his countenance showed it all over.

Terri was simply an extension of God's Love to Walter and it changed his eternal destiny!

Everything Except Love

When we don't make ***The Choice*** to let Christ live His Life out through us, however, this is what can happen...

Nancy was a missionary and part of a team of American Christians who recently smuggled Bibles across the Burmese border.

She said that the Burmese Christians had very little materially—no Bibles, no concordances, no commentaries, etc. They each had torn out pages of one old Bible that they all shared. Each of them cherished their own pages and had every word memorized. Even though the Burmese Christians were lacking in material things, she said, "The Love they displayed for each other and for us was overwhelming."

The American Christians who accompanied Nancy, however, each brought their own "personal" Bible (and sometimes a Greek or a Hebrew one besides); they each had their own concordances, different commentaries and everything materially one could desire as a Christian. But, *what was conspicuously missing among these American Christians was God's Love.* She described her Christian brothers and sisters as continually backbiting and quarreling. They had absolutely no love for each other, let alone love for the Burmese.

When the Burmese Christians left their group, the whole mission fell apart. There was no Love—no "glue"—left to hold the rest of the body together.

This, again, is a perfect example of Christian phonies, who often do more damage than good. Jesus was still in their hearts, if they were truly believers, but *self life* is what showed forth.

1 John 4:20 admonishes us, "If a man say, `I love God,' and [yet still] hateth his brother, he is a liar; for he that loveth not his brother whom he hath seen, how can he love God Whom he hath not seen?"

We Are To Initiate Love

As Christians, our only responsibility is to be *willing.* Willing *first* to love God with all of our heart, will and soul and then, willing to love others. Jesus is our example and He freely surrendered His Life so that He could be an open vessel, through which God's Love and Life could be given to us. And since 1 John 4:17 tells us, "we are to be in this world, as He is," *we*

was a "low-down-good-for-nothing slime ball" who deserved a multitude of broken bones!

A fellow Christian, however, reminded Jesse of the truth. "Jesse, you are no better than he is." "What?" Jesse said. "What are you talking about?" She thought to herself, "it's not true, I am nothing like Niles." "I am..." Then, she stopped herself and swallowed her own self-righteous pride. It was true. What goodness did she have to stand on? Her own? No way! Her only goodness came from Christ. Niles' actions *had* been rebellious and selfish and destructive, but God reminded her that He loved Niles. And, thus, what right did *she* have to judge him? "He's my child and I will take care of his rebellious ways. I simply want you to pray for him."

Jesse didn't want to do that! Her wild feelings about Niles consumed her. She was justified, by the world's standards: to look down on him and despise him. But she stopped short, took a few short breaths, and then made *The Choice* to follow God. "Okay, Lord, I choose to give You myself and all the angry emotions that I am feeling at this moment. I can't love Niles. I don't even like him. But, I know You love him and You know how to discipline him righteously and justly. Therefore, I surrender myself to You. Do what You want, I *will* just pray for him."

As she began to pray for him on a regular basis, her anger seemed to just melt away and she began to see the whole situation in a totally different light. Jesse found that the more she prayed for Niles, the more God helped her to honestly want the best for him. One day she realized God had so changed her heart, that Niles had almost become a spiritual "brother" to her and that she really *did* genuinely care about him!

When we truly learn to love God *first*, He will change our natural thoughts and feelings to match the faith choices that we have made.

The Problem: We Love Ourselves

Many Christians today want to distort the Second Commandment by saying that we must "love ourselves" *before* we can "love others." It does <u>not</u> say this. It simply says that if we are loving God first (totally giving ourselves over to Him), then *He* will enable us to love others *before or instead of ourselves*. In other words, because we have made *The Choice* to totally give ourselves over to God, He, then, is free to love His Love through us to others. This kind of self-sacrificing Love, as we have previously seen, is naturally impossible; it's only when we love (*agapao*) God (and know that He loves us) that He can pour this kind of supernatural Love through us.

Instinctively and automatically (humanely), we love (*agapao*) ourselves first, even as Christians. It's not that we have to be taught to love ourselves, we do this naturally and, this is really the root problem to begin with and what God is trying to change in all of us.

As Ephesians 5:29 tells us that, "No man ever yet hated his own flesh; but nourisheth it and cherisheth it." And, Philippians 2:21, "For all seek their own, not the things which are Jesus Christ's."

Now, some of us "totally give ourselves over" to ourselves in a prideful, boastful and arrogant way, and obviously we can see that this is wrong. But, still others of us are consumed with ourselves through self-hate, self-pity and self-abasement. This, too, is loving ourselves and, of course, not God's will. Consequently, both of these ways of loving "self" are wrong because in both cases we are consumed with our own thoughts, emotions and desires *before* God and *before* others!

Jesus wants to now reverse this natural order of things. And by our learning to love Him first, He can then fill us with His Love and enable us to love others *before or instead of ourselves*.

An Example: "If Looks Could Kill"

Here's a perfect example of a Christian totally consumed in herself—loving herself and not others.

Tracy and Sommer had known each other for years, been best of friends and now were going to the same college. Suddenly and without warning, however, Tracy was asked to leave their sorority. She was absolutely devastated, but at the same time, convinced it had to be Sommer who had told the board about her sneaking alcohol into her room. The truth was that Sommer had nothing to do with the incident. In fact, when she heard about the board's decision, she went to them and begged them to reconsider.

The following Sunday, Sommer ran into Tracy at church and gave her a big bear hug. Tracy, however, still convinced that she had betrayed her, gave her a look of "hate" that she said she will never forget. Sommer turned around and raced back to her seat. As she sat there, she could feel the hot tears streaming down her face and she wanted to run. Tracy had been her friend for such a long time, how could she ever think she was involved? Sommer could have so easily (and self righteously) told Tracy off, because she really *was* innocent. However, she stayed in her seat silently giving her hurts to God and praying not only for herself, but also for Tracy.

That afternoon, when Sommer arrived home, she continued to give her self over to the Lord and prayed that He would right the situation. The Lord prompted her to write Tracy a letter in which she lovingly explained in detail that she had nothing to do with what had happened. Tracy, by this time, however, was too self-absorbed to hear the truth. She never responded to Sommer's letter and, unfortunately, their close friendship died over the next several months. Sommer truly did her best to forgive, to initiate love and to reach out the way God would have her to do, but the door for a continued relationship was slammed shut.

It remains to be seen how long it will take for Tracy to "*stop loving herself*" and to begin to love others as God desires. Sommer is still praying, still open and still waiting.

This story, unfortunately, again seems all too common these days among Christian friends. Truly, as we said in the beginning of this book, "the Love (*Agape*) of many <u>has</u> grown cold." Like Tracy, many have made **The Choice** not to let Christ live His Life out through them, and yet, sadly, they still call themselves Christians.

The Problem: We Don't Like Ourselves

The problem is *not* that we don't love ourselves—again, we do that naturally; the basic problem is that we don't *like* ourselves. And according to Scripture, there's a world of difference between these two: "Love" is the Greek word *agapao,* which means "what we totally give ourselves over to." "Like" is the Greek word *storge* which means "what we have affection for or care for." One is a commitment love, the other is an emotional love.

Now, the reason many Christians we don't like—or have affection for—themselves is because: 1) We don't really know that God loves us personally; 2) thus, we don't have the confidence and the trust to continually lay our wills and lives down before Him and become cleansed vessels; 3) therefore, it's *not* really Christ's Life coming through us, but our own self life; and, 4) the result is, we don't "like" what we say, what we do or how we do it. And, it's no wonder—it's *not* God's Life.

So, the problem is not that we don't *love* ourselves, we do that automatically. The problem is that we don't *like* or have affection for ourselves.

Remember Tammy, "The Prom Queen," in Chapter Two. She's a perfect example of someone who didn't like or have affection for herself, and yet, she totally became consumed with herself, trying to fulfill that void in her life. She didn't like herself and yet, was totally consumed with herself.

An Example: More About Niles

We spoke about Niles just a moment ago, in our example about how God can enable us to initiate love to the unlovable.

Niles was only seventeen years old when he wanted to get a WWJD tattoo on his lower arm. Instead of wearing the bracelet that asked "What would Jesus do?," he wanted the tattoo to be right there for all to see. A friend suggested that he could make the same statement by *doing* what Jesus would do. He really didn't need a tattoo to show others he was a follower of Christ, he could show them that by his actions.

Niles, in reality, had an extremely difficult time really *doing* what Jesus would do. He really liked doing what *he* wanted to do. He didn't really want to be accountable to anyone. He would say, "God wants," when in reality it was really, "Niles wants." Thus, Niles chose his own will far too many times and ended up spiraling downward quite rapidly. The only person he ever considered was himself.

Niles' problem wasn't that he didn't love himself or that he had low self-esteem, his problem was that he really didn't *like* himself. He was handsome, smart, well-dressed, charming and had incredible musical talent, but he had an extremely difficult time feeling good about himself. And, the reason was: *he didn't really know that God loved him,* which made him unable to lay his life down to the Lord and do things *His* way. This prevented God's Life from coming through him, which resulted in his self life being shown forth—his own desires, his own pleasures, his own thoughts and emotions. Thus, down deep, he really didn't like what he did or what he said or who he had become. And, again, it's no wonder—it wasn't God's Life through him, as it should have been, but his own.

Healthy Self-Esteem

The only thing that will ever bring us that *healthy self-liking and self-esteem* that God desires is: 1) personally knowing that God loves us; 2) which will then give us the confidence to lay our wills and our lives down to Him and allow His Life to flow through us; and, 3) as a result, we'll begin to "like" what we say, what we do and how we do it because it's God's Life coming through us and not our own. (Again, see "Supplemental Study" page 162 for a *visual picture* of this.)

This is *not* self-confidence or self-esteem as the world calls it, but *God-confidence and Christ-esteem*. It's God's Life and His Character that is showing and *this* is what we like about ourselves.

An Example: Roy

Roy is a perfect example of this Godly self-confidence.

As a boy growing up in Southern California, Roy stuttered uncontrollably. His parents tried all the doctors they could find and all the methods available to overcome the problem, but to no avail. After he had become a believer, Roy told God that his supreme desire was to become a pastor and lead others to Christ. But, obviously, with his handicap, this was an impossibility.

God, nevertheless, kept impressing upon Roy's heart that if he would just learn to love Him—totally give himself over to Him—then He would enable Roy to love others by boldly preaching the Word to them. Roy clung to that promise. He committed himself to loving God with all his heart, with all his will and with all his soul, and God was faithful to keep His part of the bargain. Roy miraculously ceased stuttering, received perfectly flowing English, and began to minister.

His small Bible Study of about 20 people has now grown to over ten thousand people who come several times a week to hear him preach on Christ's gift of life and freedom. Roy is well aware that the miracle in his life has nothing at all to do with what "he has done" or what "he has accomplished," but simply with what God has done through him. Roy would be the first to tell us that the minute he gets his eyes off of the Lord and onto himself (and his own abilities), his stuttering returns. Only by *Christ-esteem* and *God-confidence*, is Roy able to minister. (Wouldn't it be wonderful if we each had such a visible indicator of our spiritual temperature?)

Only by Christ-esteem and God-confidence can any of us walk as God would have us. As Proverbs 3:26 says, "For the Lord shall be thy confidence..." (Proverbs 14:26).

We Must Live Christ's Life

People often ask us, "What is the best thing that we can do for our unbelieving family and friends?" "What book should we get them?" "What tapes should we have them listen to?" "What class would you recommend?" The answer we always give is very simple. *"Learn to make **The Choice** to let Christ live His Life out through you! Live His Love!* Show that it works for you in the bad times, as well as the good."

A Scripture that is very appropriate here is Isaiah 24:15: "...glorify the Lord in the fires." In other words, at *all* times we are to reflect and show forth Jesus' Life. It's through the humility of Jesus that God's grace reached us, therefore, it will be through our own humility—living Christ's Life—that God's grace will be able to permeate all our relationships.

Live His Forgiveness

A big part of living Christ's Life is forgiveness. And, for many of us, this presents a big stumbling block, especially if we are "justified" by the world's standards: to hold on to our own thoughts and opinions. Here's an example:

In the years since their father had remarried, Ben and his two younger teenage brothers had never really gotten along with their stepmother, Tanna. She could not understand the boys at all, and there was always a lot of tension and frustration between them. She just didn't fit into their family. She didn't like their own mother and often told them terrible stories about her. When the boys had arguments with her, Tanna would shriek and cry and always try to convince their father to be on her side.

Ben and his brothers had grown up in difficult circumstances, but had always loved God and wanted to serve Him well. They had never felt rebellious until Tanna, who was not a believer, came into their family. She seemed to be able to bring out the worst in them. She wanted to control every aspect of their lives, and sometimes they felt they would go crazy because of her stifling them.

Late one night, Ben and Tanna had a dreadful argument and Ben got kicked out of the house. He had been going to bed when Tanna came in and told him to go to his friend's house and bring back the golf clubs that he had borrowed. Ben said, "It's the middle of the night, Tanna. They're all asleep. I'll go get them tomorrow." Tanna insisted that he get up right then and go get the clubs. Ben tried again to explain that he had to get up at 5:30 in the morning, and that he was coming down with a chest cold and really needed his sleep. He would get the golf clubs the next day. "No," Tanna shouted, "go get them now!" Ben grabbed his sleeping bag and left. The next day, his dad made it clear to him that he was not wanted back in the house.

Ben's friends gave him a place to sleep for the next two weeks. They were all very supportive and had absolutely no respect for Tanna, let alone Ben's father. God, however, began to talk to Ben and said, "You need to forgive her." Ben didn't want to hear that! She had caused their family such turmoil and such misery, why, on earth, should he forgive her? *She* was the one who had forced her way into their normally contented lives.

God, however, kept prodding Ben, "What have you done to help the situation? Have you helped to bring peace to the family? Have you made Tanna feel at home?" "Well, no," he had to admit. Actually, he had openly despised Tanna, and had no respect at all for her, which, of course, didn't help his younger brothers to be obedient or respectful. Ben had never cared for Tanna, so how could he expect her to feel at home in his family? No wonder she "flipped out" so easily. He had not always been honest with her, and he had rarely considered her ideas in any of the decisions he made. Ben realized that his father's life had also been made harder because of the fighting between the two of them.

Ben felt cut to the heart at this last realization. Dad didn't need that.

So in spite of his feelings, Ben decided to make *The Choice* to do it God's way. He became willing to forgive Tanna, even though he didn't feel like it at all. And he began to pray for her. After he made the "faith" decision to forgive Tanna, the anger and the disrespect and the bitterness seemed to just fall away.

Ben took his dad to lunch and confessed some of the things that he had done in regard to Tanna. He expected his father to be angry and disappointed, but his dad was very thankful and pleased that his son was hearing from God and doing what He had asked.

Finally, he went to Tanna to ask her forgiveness for the things that God had pointed out to him. It was probably the hardest thing he ever had to do in all of his life. But, he did it because God had told him to. What blew him away, was that Tanna apologized right back, which he had not been expecting at all.

Since that day, Ben's relationship with Tanna has become far more natural. They can talk to each other pleasantly without being phony, and Ben even looks for things to do for her. She still tries in her own way to control Ben, but he recognizes that she has her own issues to deal with and that God is working in her also. He trusts God for His Love and forgiveness, and thus, she doesn't seem to get under his skin as much as she used to.

Ben is an example of *real* Christianity. Again, the Life is always Jesus', but **The Choice** to implement it, is constantly ours.

Walk Wisely in God's Love

Unconditionally loving others does not mean "sloppy Agape" or unbalanced Love. *Love without God's Wisdom alongside is not God's Love at all.* God's Wisdom is what will teach us *how* to walk in God's Love wisely. Only God has the right solution for each situation we face and we need to continually seek Him for that direction.

As mentioned earlier, God's Love can manifest itself mercifully in our lives, or it can manifest itself in strictness and firmness, when needed. The question becomes, which type of Love do we use for our particular situation—God's longsuffering and merciful Love, or His severe and disciplinary Love? Both are God's Love, but in our own unique situation, which kind of Love do we use? Again, we need God's Wisdom on this. Every person and every situation is different and what works for one is not necessarily what will work in the next circumstance. Only God can tell us how to love *wisely*.

God's Wisdom will teach us when to love in mercy and compassion and when to love in strictness and firmness. As we said, each situation, each circumstance and each person is different. Only God has the perfect answers we need, because only He has the Love we need and the Power to perform that Love in our lives.

Loving others with *Agape* Love does *not* mean overlooking the sin that they are involved in, pretending that it doesn't exist or taking responsibility for it by pointing it out and trying to fix it ourselves. When we love someone wisely with God's Love, we still see the sin in their lives, but we don't take it upon ourselves to bring it up all the time. We simply give our feelings about the sin to God and then *trust Him* to do something about it.

Thus, it's *not* our responsibility to point out another's faults. Nothing will turn others off quicker than our being a Holy Spirit "nagger." God has not called us to be "criticizers," but encouragers. We are not to constantly pick at our loved ones, but simply to trust God and love them wisely. We obey Him by giving Him all of our frustrations, resentments and bitterness, and we trust Him by knowing He will pour His wise Love through us.

Be a Hosea

Hosea in the Old Testament is a powerful example of one who loved others as God designed. He loved God by continually surrendering his life 'o that God's Life might be shown through him. He didn't overlook the sin that his wife was involved in, but God enabled him to forgive her and to love her wisely. In his own power and ability, Hosea could *never* have loved his rebellious family the way that he did. Yet, because of his faithfulness to love God first, yielding his will and life completely, God enabled him to unconditionally and wisely love his wife and children. When we allow God to live His Life out through us, as did Hosea, what they will see in us is God.

The question: "Are you willing to be a Hosea?" Are you willing to lay your will and life down so that God can reach your family, your friends and the Laurens of this world through you?

"To Them That Perish, It's Foolishness"

This way of living, of course, looks crazy to the world. It's totally opposite to everything we have ever learned and everything we have ever been taught! Thus, to the world, it's completely foolish!

And, of course, they are right. This is a foolish way of living, because it is *not* natural! It's *not* a normal, human response. In fact, it's completely opposite to our instinctive, self-centered ways of thinking and reacting. God, Himself, tells us that "the preaching of the cross is to them that perish foolishness; but unto us which are saved it is the power of God" (1 Corinthians 1:18). And, it's the same thing with His way of Life. To them who don't know God's supernatural Life, living like this seems very foolish. But to them who see God work "impossible miracles," when they are willing to lay down their wills and their lives, this way is not only the power of God working, it's our whole purpose for living.

As someone wrote recently, "As I am beginning to understand and live God's Way of Love, I'm alive for the first time in my life."

God's Life through us is the only thing that will bring our families, our friends and our relatives to Christ. It's His lovingkindness—in spite of the circumstances, in spite of how we feel and in spite of what we think—that is going to draw them. However, we will only be able to mirror and reflect on the outside, the Love we are intimately and genuinely experiencing on the inside. In other words, if we are not experiencing God's personal Love for ourselves—either because of doubt or a wall of frustrations and hurts—then we are not going to be able to pass that Love and that Life on to others.

What Will You Choose?

How about you? What will you choose? Will you live Life as God designed or will you settle for a pale and phony imitation of Christianity, like Lauren's friends? God yearns that you might *choose Life* and by so doing, become a *real* Christian!

"Today, I have given you ***The Choice*** between life and death, between blessings and curses....Oh, that you would *choose Life* so that you might live" (Deuteronomy 30:19).

Can you tear up that long list of justified hurts and wrongs that others have done? Can you unconditionally forgive that person who has hurt you over and over again? Can you lay aside all those things and, for the hundredth time, choose to yield yourself to God and let Him love them through you?

There's no way in the world we can love like this naturally. Only God can love like this through us supernaturally. And it's only as we yield ourselves—all our negative thoughts, emotions and desires that are contrary to His—and make *The Choice* to become an open vessel that He can love like this *through us*.

What choice will you make?

Questions from Chapter Four

1) Self-esteem and self-confidence are such popular themes today, how is it possible to have the proper God-confidence and Christ-esteem that God wants?

2) In your own words, define the difference between the Biblical word *love* and the secular word *like*. Give examples of each.

3) What does it mean to be an extension of God's Life? If we ourselves are hurting, how can we do this? Give an example in your own life where someone was an extension of God's Love to you.

4) Do you know people who love themselves in a self-pity or self-hate way? How about in a prideful way? Which do you do?

5) What *other part* of God's character must go along side of His Love in our lives? How can we genuinely love those who have hurt or betrayed us? How can God really expect us to love our enemies? (See "Supplemental Study" page 162 for a *visual picture* of this.)

* If you want the suggested answers to these questions, they are available on our website **www.kingshighway.org**, under the *Plain and Simple Series*, or you can write us at the address on the back of this book, or call us.

Conclusion
Now It's Your Turn

In conclusion, Jesus is the mediator or the vessel of God's Life to us. He died expressly so that His Love and His Life might be released *through Him* to us (1 John 4:10). His whole purpose and ministry was to willingly lay down His Life so that we might receive the Father's Love. And, as Christians, this is our calling also. To make the constant choice to lay down our lives so that Jesus might give His Love and Life to others *through us*.

This is what makes Christianity so completely different from all the other religions of the world. Our God is tangible, touchable and reachable, because He not only lives in us, *He will live His Life out through us*. God's purpose is that we might not only experience His Love for ourselves, but that we might become an open vessel to pass that Love and that Life on to others. "Hereby perceive we the Love of God, because He laid down His Life for us: and we ought to lay down our lives for our brethren" (1 John 3:16).

When Jesus walked the earth, He was a true representation of God's Love and Life. He not only loved His own, He also loved His enemies (Luke 6: 27, 32, 35). He knew that perfect balance between God's merciful Love and His strict and disciplinary Love. And, as we lay down our wills and our lives to Him, He promises to pour that same Love and that same Life through us to all of our relationships.

Your Turn

Now it's your turn. Have you *chosen Life*? Have you responded to God's Love? Have you said, "Yes, God, I need Your Love. I need Your forgiveness. I want You to be my Life itself."

If not, you can determine your eternal destiny—right now—in the privacy of your own will, by simply asking Christ to come into your heart and to take over. This commitment will launch you on the Grandest Adventure of all and is the very reason you are here reading this, right now.

Accepting God into our hearts and knowing that He will love us unconditionally is the foundation pad upon which our whole spiritual house is going to be built. We can't go further in learning how to love and be loved as God designed, until we *first* know that we belong to Him, and that He has the central place in our hearts. We must know that Jesus is in our hearts loving us *before* we can have the confidence to lay our wills and our lives down, moment by moment, and love Him in return.

The meaning of life lies in our relationships: first our relationship with God, then our relationship with others. By our first loving God with all our heart, will and soul, we not only will experience His Love for ourselves, but we'll be enabled to pass on that Love to others.

The Choice

God has given us a continual choice: to either let Christ live His Life out through us, or to close ourselves off to God and rely upon our own power and ability to live the Christian Life.

This is God's challenge to you: ***Choose Life*** (learn to live as God designed) so that you may have that abundant Life He has planned for you. If you refuse to take God's challenge and don't choose Life, then, as Scripture says, you will encounter many problems and live a very empty and meaningless life (Deuteronomy 30:19).

The truth is that only Jesus has the abundant Life that we need. All we must do is, moment by moment, make ***The Choice*** to love Him so that His Life from our hearts can shine through us. (See page 162 in "Supplemental Study" for *visual picture* of this.)

It doesn't matter how long we have been Christians, how often we go to church, how many Scriptures we know or how sincere our prayers are, *authentic Christianity* is simply recognizing our own sin and self, and then choosing to surrender these things to Him so that He can live His Life out through us.

Again, it's God's Life—but our choice to accept it—and our choice to, moment by moment, pass it on.

As Matthew 7:14 says, "Strait is the gate, and narrow is the way, which leads to *Life*, and [only a] few will find it."

The question is: Will you be one who does?

it was actually destroyed. And finally, Solomon's Temple was special because it was the only temple in which the Ark of the Covenant rested. None of the other temples contained the Ark.

Thus, in order for us to understand what we look like *internally* and what it means to love God with all our heart, mind and soul, we are going to compare our bodies (as the Temple of God now) to the actual layout and structure of Solomon's Temple way back in the Old Testament. And, by doing so, hopefully we will gain a better understanding not only of ourselves, but also what the terms "heart," "mind" and "soul" really mean. God is a God of extreme detail and precision and there is something very special and unique meant by each of these words. Therefore, in order to love Him the way that He intends, we need to understand *His* meanings for each of these concepts.

As you begin to grasp some of God's concepts in this section, we hope you come away with an awe that *everything* He has put in the Bible is there by design. Not one small detail is meaningless. It's a fascinating study and we hope you get as excited as we are over what you are about to learn. (Should you want to delve further into this material, you might want to pick up our book *Be Ye Transformed*, which has much more information.)

We are praying that as you see yourself in these charts, you will not only gain a better understanding of what happens when God's Life freely flows through you, but also, you will see just what happens when you block or quench His Spirit and stop that flow of Life.

CHART 1: The Elevation View

Chart 1 is the front elevation view of Solomon's Temple. You can see how the main sanctuary rested on a raised platform. The Temple itself consisted of the Holy of Holies in the rear ᴬ; the Holy Place in the middle ᴮ; and the Porch ᶜ, with its two pillars in the front ᴰ, facing the Inner and Outer Courts ᶠ.

Be sure to note the side wings on either side of the main sanctuary ᴱ. These were secret, hidden, wooden chambers that were supposed to be used for storing the priests' worship items used in the Holy Place and also the historical records of Israel. We'll see in a moment, however, what was actually stored there.

CHART 2: The Floor Plan View (see next page)

This is the actual floor plan of Solomon's Temple. You can see that the main sanctuary was made up of the Holy of Holies [A] in the rear, the Holy Place [B] in the middle, and the Porch [C] in the front.

Surrounding the sanctuary were secret, hidden, wooden chambers [E], where the priests were supposed to store the worship items for the Holy Place and the treasures and trophies of Israel, to remind them of all that God had done for them. It was here, however, that the priests actually stored their own personal idolatrous worship items, thinking that because they were hidden and out of sight, *no one would see and no one would know* (Ezekiel 8:6-12).

In front of the two main doors to the Porch, but still considered a part of the Porch, were two Bronze Pillars [D]. Stepping down seven steps was the Inner Court [H] and on an even lower level, the Outer Court [I].

The Choice

The Temple of God

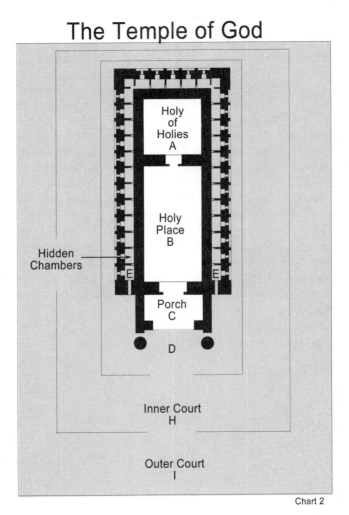

Chart 2

"Blueprint" of a Believer

CHART 3: The Spiritual View (see page 147)

Now, let's study the Temple as a model or a blueprint of a New Testament Believer (i.e., one who has the Holy Spirit dwelling within).

The Holy of Holies is analogous to a believer's **spirit** (the Greek word is *pneuma*) [1]; the Holy Place represents his **heart** (the Greek word is *kardia*) [2]; the Porch is analogous to his **willpower** or volition (the Greek word is *dianoia*) [3].

[Note: In the Greek language there are 13 different words that are simply translated "mind." One of these Greek words is *dianoia*, which is the one used in the First Commandment—"love God with all your mind." More precisely translated, the word *dianoia* really means "willpower" (or "volition"). It's our will and the power to perform our will. Thus, from now on, whenever we refer to the First Commandment, we will call *dianoia* "will or willpower" (rather than mind) in order to be more specific and to avoid confusion. Consequently, the first commandment should read that we are to love God with all our heart, with all our willpower and with all our soul.]

The secret, wooden chambers around the main sanctuary represents the **hidden part of a believer's soul** (the Hebrew word is *cheder*) [6]—the part of our soul where we store our hurts, doubts, and fears thinking that because they are hidden, *no one will see, no one will know,* just like the priest's did.

The Inner Court represents the **conscious part of a man's soul** (the Greek word is *psyche*) [4]; and the Outer Court represents his **body** (the Greek word is *soma*) [5]. Our soul and body together (all the grey area on the chart) represent our *flesh*.

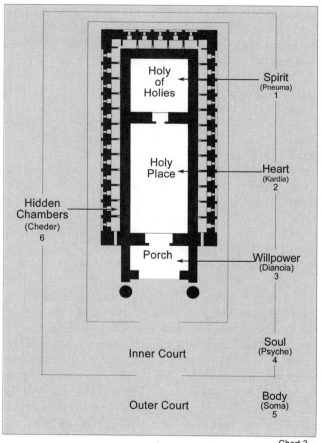

Chart 3

Turn to **CHART 4** (see page 150)

As we said, *before* we can learn to love God in the way He desires, with all our heart, will and soul, we must *first* understand what each of these terms really means. Thus, in **Chart 4**, we'll first give an overview and define these words, then, we'll come back and explore, in detail, what it means to love Him with each.

OUR NEW SPIRIT [1]

As a born-again believer (one who has asked Jesus to take control of his life), the spirit that now dwells at the core of our being is not our "old" human spirit anymore, but a totally *new* spirit given to us by God at our new birth. Being "born again" simply means receiving a totally *new life source* or *power source,* i.e., God's Spirit. God has united our spirit with His, and we have become one spirit with Him, just as 1 Corinthians 6:17 says. "He that is joined unto the Lord is one spirit [with Him]."

God's Spirit, now united with our spirit, is like the new energy source or power source of our lives. It's somewhat analogous to a generator or an electric power unit in a huge building. Without the generator's energy and power, nothing in the building will operate. And, it's the same with us. Without our new spirit, our bodies will not have any life at all. Our new spirit is a *life-giving power* source that quickens us, makes us alive and gives us life. Its removal means death.

Our new spirit can be compared to an electric light. In order to have light, however, Psalm 18:28 tells us that our spirit must be united with the Spirit of God. It says that God is the One who "lights the candle of our spirit." In other words, the Spirit of God is like the *Master Transformer* that fills our own spirit with His Light. Our spirit, then, simply becomes the *transmitter of that Light*. Apart from God's Spirit igniting our spirit, our lives would remain dark.

OUR NEW HEART [2]

Our *new* heart is the actual place where *God's Life*—His supernatural Love, Wisdom and Power—is created, started and brought into "new" existence by God's Spirit. As God says in Ezekiel 36:26-27, "A *new* heart also will I give [create in] you, and a *new* spirit will I put within you...I will take away the stony heart [old heart] out of your flesh, and I will give you a heart of flesh [a new, living heart]."

This "heart of flesh," is *not* our old heart simply changed or renewed, but a brand new heart, something that wasn't there before. In other words, when we are born again, God replaces our "old" human heart life (our "natural" love, wisdom and power) with *His* brand-new heart life [7].

Our new heart life is "*Christ in [us]*, our hope of glory" (Colossians 1:27, emphasis added).

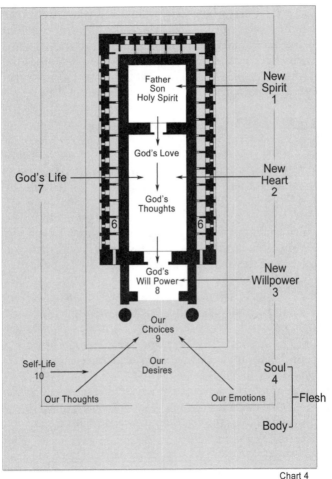

Chart 4

An Example: Prisoner in Sydney

Here's a wonderful story about the new spirit and new heart that God gives us as a result of being born again.

Several years ago, when we were ministering in Australia, a woman came up and told us a true story about a friend of hers. She said her friend's husband had always been very jealous of his wife. One time, he exploded over some minor incident, and literally tried to kill his wife. He was put in jail, but managed to escape, and while his wife was recuperating in the hospital, he once again, attempted to kill her. In a fit of rage, he tried to rip her large wedding ring off her finger and in the process, bent the ring completely out of shape.

Again he was caught, only this time he was placed in a maximum security prison. During the years he was there, someone shared Christ with him. He recognized his need, accepted Jesus into his heart and became born again with a new spirit and a new nature—God's new Life.

At that particular time, someone sent him *The Way of Agape* tapes. Through these tapes, God revealed to this man that he was a new creation in Christ, and that he now had God's supernatural Life within him to give out. The man's life radically changed, and he became devoted to reading God's Word.

Some months later, when he was released from prison, he looked up his ex-wife. After a period of time, in which I'm sure she was very scared of him, they began to date again and eventually, he led her to Christ. They were remarried, and she now wears that broken, bent-out-of-shape wedding ring around her neck as a symbol of the miracle that God performed in their lives.

"If any man be in Christ, he is a new creature: old things are passed away; behold, ALL things have become new [brand-new spirit, brand-new Love, brand-new Thoughts, and brand-new Power]" (2 Corinthians 5:17).

"Old" Human Heart Is Corrupt

Scripture tells us that our old, human heart *before* we are born again (before we receive God's Spirit) is evil and corrupt from birth (Genesis 8:21). It tells us that our old heart, no matter what we do or try, will always be self-centered, proud, and going its own way. It will never, on its own, seek God.

Even in the New Testament, wherever the corruptness of our heart is mentioned, it always refers to our old, human-heart life *before* the Spirit of God comes to dwell within us permanently. In other words, before God lights the candle of our spirit.

Even if we could understand the corruptness of our old heart, Scripture tells us that the worst part of all is that *no one knows how to cure it*. In other words, it's incurable! Thus, without God's intervention in our lives, there's no hope for any change. There's no cure—there's no remedy!

An Example: Nothing Helped Till Jesus

Heather was a beautiful girl who absolutely adored her family, until drugs ravaged her life. Her parents loved her and didn't want to let her destroy herself. So, they spent thousands upon thousands of dollars trying to cure her. They sent her to psychiatric hospitals, care units, drug rehab hospitals, etc. But, nothing ever seemed to help. Some of these hospitals cost her family over $5000 a week. Her parents were so desperate; however, they spared no expense in trying to find a cure. They tried every psychiatrist, every therapist, and every counselor they could find. However, nothing ever touched or changed this girl's life—until she met Jesus.

When the Spirit of God came inside Heather's heart, she not only received a new power source (a new Spirit), she also received "new life" itself (a new heart). Now, she had God's Power within her, giving her the capability for real and lasting internal change. She no longer had to rely upon her own natural human ability for change which, as we all know, will always let us down. She now had God's Spirit within her for real and lasting change.

This is why we all need, not only a new spirit (a new power source), but also a new heart so that God's new Life itself can begin to come forth. Again, "If any man be in Christ, he is a new creature: old things are passed away; behold, *all* things are become new."

God's Life in Our Hearts

Thus, our old heart, which Scripture tells us is evil (incurable and unknowable) from birth, is totally replaced by a brand-new heart when we are born again by God's Spirit. This brand new heart contains God's Life which is totally pure, completely incorruptible, and entirely holy *because it's God's Life,* not our own.

This new heart Life is called the "hidden man of the heart," and is the center core or the true essence of our being. Upon this foundation everything else in our lives is going to be built, and upon which all continuing activity will depend. This is the solid rock that we talked about in the first chapter. It's "God in us," our hope of glory.

Again, it's important that we understand that this message of Life will *not* work *unless* we are "born again," with a new spirit and a new heart. Only then will we have the supernatural Life of God within us for real and lasting change.

<u>OUR NEW WILLPOWER [3]</u>

Again, on **CHART 4** (page 150)

Now, the most critical area of all is the <u>new</u> willpower that we receive as a result of being born again. As we said earlier, the Greek word *dianoia* means "our will and the power to perform it." Interestingly, *dia* means "channel" and *noya* means "of the mind" or "of the spirit." Our willpower is exactly that. It's the channel or conduit through which

God's Spirit flows from our hearts out into our lives. You can see on the chart its strategic importance. It's like the passageway, the doorway or the gateway for God's Life to get to our souls. This passageway or doorway can be "opened" so God's Life can flow unhindered, or it can be "closed" and thus, God's Life quenched and blocked.

Our willpower (or our choice point) is really the "key" to our whole Christian walk because what we choose, moment by moment, determines *whose* "life" will be lived in our souls—God's or our own.

Note on the chart that our new willpower really has two distinct parts to it. First, we have *God's supernatural Will and Power* [8], given to us as a part of our new birth. This is where *God counsels us as to what His will is*, and then, where *He gives us the supernatural Power to perform that will* in our lives. The second part of our willpower, however, is something I wish that God had left out of my own makeup. This is *our own free choice* [9]—the freedom to choose to follow what God has shown me and trust in His Power to perform it in my life; or, the freedom to choose to do what I think, feel, and desire, and then trust in my own ability and power to perform that choice in my life.

Our Choice

Our choice is the most crucial and the most vital function of our entire makeup. Our lives depend upon our moment-by-moment choices.

As Christians, as we have said before, we are continually faced with ***The Choice*** to let Christ live His Life out through us; or, to depend upon our own power and ability to live. In other words, we can make a *"faith choice"* (a non-feeling choice to do what God has told us, regardless of how we feel) and let God's Life come from our hearts out into our lives; or, we can make an *"emotional choice"* (to do what *we* feel, what *we* think and what *we* desire) and quench God's Life in our heart.

The way we make faith choices is simply by giving our *sin* and *self* to God (as we learned last chapter) and by saying, "not my will, but Thine" (Matthew 26:39). These are choices we make by faith, not our feelings. When we make emotional choices (choices prompted by our feelings), however, we'll end up playing right into the Enemy's hands.

An Example: Wendy

Here's a perfect example that illustrates the power of our choices.

Wendy, a beautiful friend of mine, had to travel on business from Durango, Colorado, to the next town which was at least 40 miles away. This part of Colorado is spectacularly beautiful, but very sparsely populated. Between Durango and the next town, there is absolutely nothing.

Wendy had just received *The Way of Agape* audio tapes a few weeks previously and she thought this long drive would be a perfect opportunity to finish them. However, she became so engrossed in what she was hearing on the tapes (about making moment-by-moment "faith" choices), that she didn't realize she was nearly out of gas and had long driven past the last gas station in Durango. There would not be another station for 40 miles.

Sure enough, about 15 or 20 miles outside of Durango, she ran out of gas. The car literally stopped. She pulled over to the side of the road and became scared to death as she realized her precarious predicament. Since she was going to a business appointment, she was all dressed up (heels and all), so there was no way she could walk any distance. And even if she could have, there was no place to go for help. The few cars that <u>did</u> pass her, terrified her. They were mostly men with beards and long hair, driving 4 x 4 trucks with shot guns racked in their rear windows.

As she sat there contemplating her situation, God impressed upon her heart what she had been listening to on the tapes—about making faith choices (non-feeling choices) to trust God in all circumstances. She realized that this applied to her predicament now and that she too had a choice. She could either panic and become paralyzed with fear (which she was already beginning to experience), or she could make *faith choices,* releasing God's Life and His Wisdom from her heart.

She decided to try the latter. By faith, she chose to give God her fear and to trust Him to protect her and give her the wisdom she needed to get through this situation. After her prayer, God impressed it upon her to try the ignition one more time. She gently turned it on and, surprisingly, the motor sputtered and then started. She was ecstatic! She put the car into first gear and crept down the highway. The farther she went, the more elated she became. God had heard her prayers and He was now performing a miracle right before her eyes.

Believe it or not, my friend drove that "empty" tank the whole 20 miles to the next city. She told me later that when she would come to a hill, she simply made more faith choices to trust God, softly stepped on the gas pedal and there always seemed to be just enough "oomph" to make it over the hill.

When she finally did arrive at the next city, she stopped at the first gas station feeling absolutely overjoyed. The gas station attendant even asked her if she was all right, because she looked so radiant (light-filled!). Thus, she was able to witness to him as she told him the whole story.

Wendy made it to her appointment, obviously a little late, but nevertheless, safely. She had learned an incredible lesson about God's faithfulness. Now, I don't recommend going out of town without gas and putting God to the test. But, to me, this is a perfect example of the importance of making constant faith choices to trust God in all situations. When we do this, we free Him to perform miracles in our lives, just like He did in Wendy's.

Our willpower is critical because what we choose, moment by moment, not only determines the direction of our lives, but also *whose* life will be lived in our souls—either God's or our own!

As we said, it's always His Life in our hearts, but our continual choice to implement it in our souls.

<u>OUR SOUL</u> [4]

Continue on **CHART 4** (page 150)

We can define our souls as a *neutral area* that is either going to be filled with God's Life from our hearts (if we have made faith choices), or filled with self life, if we have quenched God's Life by making emotional choices. Our souls are made up of our natural, human life: our own thoughts, emotions and desires. This is our "self life" [10] that we have so often referred to and that God wants continually surrendered to Him.

Now, there is a hidden, secret part of our soul—those secret chambers [6]—where we push down and bury our hurts, bitterness, unforgivenesses, etc., if we don't know what else to do with them. And, we'll talk more about this area in just a moment.

For simplicity's sake, think of our souls as the *outward* or "visible" part of our lives. In other words, our souls are what we see, feel and hear coming from one another. We can't see each other's hearts, only God can do that. What we see is each other's "souls."

The best analogy I can think of to show you the difference between heart life and soul life is with plants in a garden. *Heart life* is like the root life of those plants. It's underground, we can't see it, but nevertheless, it's essential to the health and growth of the plants above. *Soul life*, on the other hand, is like the beautiful flowers that grow above the ground. The flowers are the direct result of the health of the root life. We can visibly see the flowers, smell them, feel them and touch them. Jeremiah 31:12 even says, "[Our] soul [should] be as a watered garden."

So, again, think of our soul as being a *"neutral area"* that is either going to be filled with God's Life from our hearts (*flowers*), if we have made faith choices; or self life (*weeds*), if we have quenched God's Life by making emotional choices.

Let's see visibly how this works.

Turn to CHART 5 (page 162)

Ideally, if we have made faith choices [9], our souls *will* show forth God's Life [7] from our hearts. In other words, His *Agape* Love [11] in our hearts becomes our Love [12] out in our souls, His Wisdom [13] in our hearts becomes our thoughts [14] out in our souls, and His Will [8] becomes our will [16] in our lives.

Remember, we said that to love God meant to totally give ourselves over to Him so that we almost become one. Well, **Chart 5** is a perfect, visual picture of a person *loving God with all their heart, will and soul*. (They have become one.)

This is what a *real* Christian looks like inside, because he has made ***The Choice*** to let Christ live His Life out through him.

Now, notice that the light coming from this temple looks like a *flashlight*. This is what Luke 11:33 means when he says, "No man, when he hath lighted a lamp (candle), putteth it in a secret place, neither under a bushel, but *on a lampstand, that they who come in may see the light*."

So, our soul can either show God's Life (His Light) from our hearts (**Chart 5**) or:

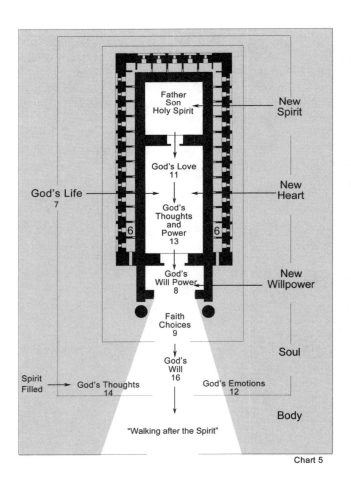

Chart 5

Turn to **CHART 6** (page 165)

If we have chosen to follow our own thoughts, emotions, and desires[9] over what God has prompted [8], then, we'll end up quenching God's Spirit [18] and showing forth "self life" [10].

Chart 6 is a visual picture of a person who is *not* loving God with all his heart, will and soul and one who is *not* an open vessel for His Life. This is what a phony Christian looks like internally, because he has made *The Choice* not to let Christ live His Life out through him. Stand back from this picture for a moment and see if you can see the "ugly face" and the frown that is portrayed. I never saw it before, but when I teach this class and project this picture up on a screen, this is what the audience seems to see. Do you see it?

Notice also that the light in this temple is blocked or quenched from showing. This is what Luke 11:33 means when God says, "No man [should], when he hath lighted a lamp (candle), *putteth it in a secret place, neither under a bushel....*" God's Light is certainly "covered over and hidden" in this Christian individual.

Where Does Self Life Come From?

Let me ask you a question. If we have God's Life in our hearts [7] and this is now our true nature, where does our *self life* [10] come from? Where do our negative thoughts, emotions and desires originate from? Where are they triggered from?

Self life comes from the hurts, resentments, doubts, pride, bitterness, etc. that we have never properly dealt with, and have instead, stuffed and buried in those secret, hidden chambers (6) of our soul, thinking that *no one will know, no one will see* (just like those priests did way back in Solomon's day). Self life is triggered when we choose to follow what those "buried" things are telling us to do (see the black arrows #21), <u>over</u> what God is prompting us to do [8].

With this in mind, here's an interesting analogy someone wrote us about the hidden chambers.

I envision the roots of my "self life" to be like those deep underground rock vaults that hold nuclear waste. At the bottom of the granite rock vaults is a concentration of deadly elements (possibly plutonium) that are cracking the vaults and leaking the poison waste into the river and ocean systems.

It's true, as we allow that poisonous waste (things from our hidden chambers) to leak out, they *will* crack our very foundation and contaminate everything that we think, say and do.

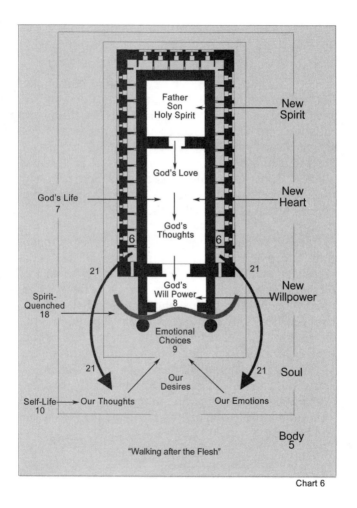

Chart 6

An Example: "I Long to be Free"

Here's an example of how things in our hidden chambers affect our lives.

Tom came to know Christ when he was 13.

He had grown up in a very volatile household, but had vowed never to repeat the things that he had seen his father do. And yet, as he was older, the anger, bitterness and unforgiveness that characterized his father was exactly how he was beginning to behave. He hated himself for it. At times, he even became suicidal because he felt like such a hypocrite, loving the Lord on the one hand, and yet, not being able to control his emotions on the other.

He ended up getting his girlfriend pregnant and thus, added a huge load of guilt on top of the anger, confusion and insecurity that he already felt. At the least provocation, he would violently explode. The terrible memories of his childhood and the fights between his mom and dad, constantly plagued him. He couldn't help remembering the times when he had tried to be a referee between them and save his mom. He longed to be free of all these memories, but didn't know how. He felt like he was his own prisoner, desperately trying to escape himself, only to be met with failure again and again. He hated the person he had become, yet didn't know a way out.

Tom's letter ends with, "I *long* to let these feelings go, but I just don't know where to begin."

Our Hidden Chambers

Things that happen to us in the past that are painful and traumatic will *not* go away on their own. And, unless we know "how" to give these things to God, we'll end up just like Tom, pushing them down into our hidden chambers where they will eventually affect what we feel, how we think and how we act.

God wants these hidden chambers, in His timing and in His way, to be cleansed, healed and then filled with God's Truth (His Word). Once they are cleansed and the *roots* removed, then the *symptoms* (the outward thoughts and emotions that we can see) will not occur again. The way the roots are removed is by going through the four essential steps that we learned last chapter—how we give things to God. (Again, if you want more information in this area, *Be Ye Transformed* has all the details.)

So, self life (the anger, unforgiveness, bitterness, etc.) is triggered by the negative things we have *never* given over to God, but, instead, have simply stored in the hidden chambers of our soul. These hidden chambers are a part of our "flesh" (all the grey area on the charts) and this is the area that God is highlighting in each of our lives, trying to teach us how to make *The Choice* to surrender these things to Him. It's called the sanctification process. We give God our self, He gives us His Self—His Life.

"Always bearing about in the body the dying of the Lord Jesus, that the life also of Jesus might be made manifest in our body. For we which live are always delivered unto death for Jesus' sake, [so] that *the life also of Jesus might be made manifest in our mortal flesh*" (2 Corinthians 4:10-11).

OUR BODY [5]

Continue on **CHART 6** (page 165)

We said earlier that our body can be compared to the Outer Court of Solomon's Temple. The Outer Court, which was on an even lower level than the Inner Court, was constantly exposed to many "outside" influences. King Solomon's own palace opened up into the Outer Court. There he housed his 700 wives (yes, 700 wives) and, adjacent to the Outer Court he had his harem buildings, where it is said that he kept as many as 300 concubines. (Talk about outside influences!)

1 Kings 11:1-6 tells us that it was these foreign wives (and playmates) and their ungodly influence that turned Solomon's heart away from following the Lord. He wasn't careful to love the Lord with all his heart, will and soul as his father, David, had done.

In Jesus' day, the Outer Court was the place where the money changers and the dove sellers were allowed. Even Satan himself tempted Jesus from the pinnacle of the Outer Court. Just think in our own lives of all the outside influences that continually try to quench God's Spirit in us and draw us away from wholeheartedly following God (television, movies, internet, magazines, advertisements, friends and family, etc.).

If we choose to *walk after the Spirit* (**Chart 5**) by making faith choices, our bodies will show God's Life from our hearts. If, however, we choose to *walk after the flesh* (**Chart 6**) by making emotional choices, our bodies will reflect our own self life.

Why Hypocrisy Occurs

Therefore, we can be Christians all our lives, yet because we continue to make *emotional choices* that quench God's Life in us, no one will ever know that we are believers at all. God's Life in us will be blocked, and no one will ever see the difference between our life and that of our neighbors down the street who don't even know God.

Chart 6 is exactly what a *hypocrite* looks like. He "says" that he is a Christian and yet his "life" shows forth something totally different—fig leaves! And, looking at the chart you can see just how this happens. Christ's Life is *still* in his heart, but it's blocked from coming forth by his own sin and self. This is why so many in the Christian body are having such a difficult time. We are living two lives! We *say* one thing, and yet *our lives* show something else.

We pray that by seeing these blueprints of our architectural makeup, you not only will understand why hypocrisy occurs, but also how to make *The Choice* to prevent it.

God Wants Us to Be "Spirit Filled"

Just as Solomon's Temple in 1 Kings 8:10-11 and 2 Chronicles 5:13-14 was filled from the *inside out* with God's Spirit as He came forth from the Holy of Holies and filled the Temple, this is exactly God's purpose for each of us. Daily, as we choose to surrender ourselves and love God with all our heart, will and soul, His Spirit can freely issue forth from the Holy of Holies of our hearts and fill our souls and our bodies with His Life and His Glory. (Review **Chart 5**)

As 1 Corinthians 6:20 declares, "For ye are bought with a price: therefore glorify [be filled with, reflect, manifest and shine forth] God in your body."

This filling, as we have seen, is *not* a one-time event, however. Nor is it automatic. It's a moment-by-moment choice to love God and to stay filled with His Spirit. "Be ye not unwise, but understanding what the will of the Lord is. [That ye] be [*being*] filled with the Spirit [all day long, every day]" (Ephesians 5: 17-18).

The question is: Do others see Jesus' Light (His Life) in you?

Questions from Supplemental Study

1) Do the charts in this chapter help you to visualize yourself *internally*? In your own words describe the difference between our heart and our soul. Why is this so important to understand? Where does our "self life" come from?

2) Can you give a personal example of an incident where something triggered negative emotions or thoughts that you thought you had previously dealt with, but you probably only pushed down into the hidden chambers. How should you now deal with it?

3) In light of these charts, can you now explain why hypocrisy occurs?

4) If we really can't correct or fix our "self life" (our own thoughts, emotions and desires that are contrary to God's), what are we to do with it? Describe in your own words, the steps we need to take.

* If you want the suggested answers to these questions, they are available on our website **www.kingshighway.org**, under the *Plain and Simple Series*, or you can write us at the address on the back of this book, or call us.

PLAIN AND SIMPLE SERIES®

The Key
HOW TO LET GO AND LET GOD
This book teaches us the moment-by-moment steps to letting go of ourselves, our circumstances and others and putting on Christ. It gives us a practical guide to giving our problems to God and leaving them there. This is one of our most popular books.

(121 pages, $6.95, ISBN 978-0-9753593-0-3)

Why Should I be the First to Change?
THE KEY TO A LOVING MARRIAGE
This is the story of the amazing "turnaround" of Chuck and Nancy's 20-year Christian marriage which reveals the dynamic secret that releases the power of God's Love already resident in every believer. Riveting, yet easy reading.

(119 pages, $6.95, ISBN 978-0-9753593-1-0)

Tomorrow May Be Too Late
DISCOVERING OUR DESTINY
A simple, non-threatening and easy to read book that chronicles God's whole plan for mankind. In just a little over a hundred pages, it relates man's spiritual journey from the beginning of time to the very end, showing how God has been personally and intimately involved all along. Perfect for non-believers.

(155 pages, $6.95, ISBN 978-0-9745177-8-0)

The Choice
HYPOCRISY OR REAL CHRISTIANITY
As Christians, we are faced with a constant choice: either to live our Christian life in our own power and ability, or to set ourselves aside and let Christ live His Life out through us. Written especially for youth.

(171 pages, 6.95, ISBN 978-0-615-34892-6)

Against the Tide
GETTING BEYOND OURSELVES
This little book gives the practical tools we need to implement "faith choices" in our lives. These are choices that set aside our natural thoughts and emotions, and allow us to love and be loved as God desires. Great for understanding our emotions.

(172 pages, $5.95, ISBN 978-0-9745177-0-4)

Never Give Up!
THE FRUIT OF LONGSUFFERING
Most of us talk very openly about the need to "be like Christ" and to have His characteristics of Love, joy, peace, but what about the fruit of longsuffering—the determination never to give up? God promises us that He will strengthen us; help us and uphold us. (Isaiah 41:10) The question is: How do we, like Paul, patiently endure our trials? This little book gives us the answers!

(224 pages, $6.95, ISBN 978-0-9760994-1-3)

Additional Resources

UNDERSTANDING GOD'S LOVE

Personal Application Workbook
DVD Series (7 Sessions)
DVD Bible Study Package
Leader's Guide
CD Audio
MP3 Audio

1-866-775-KING

On the Internet:
http://www.kingshighway.org

The King's HIGH Way

UNDERSTANDING GOD'S TRUTH

In this sequel to *The Way of Agape*, Chuck and Nancy teach us the practical application of renewing our minds. Only in *putting off* our fears, anxieties, depression, anger, and unbelief and *putting on* Christ can we be free to reflect Him in all we do. Outlines at the back of each chapter contain all the Scriptural references.

Additional Resources:

Textbook
Personal Application Workbook
DVD Series (7 Sessions)
DVD Bible Study Package
Leader's Guide
CD Audio
MP3 Audio

1-866-775-KING

On the Internet:
http://www.kingshighway.org

The King's HIGH Way

UNDERSTANDING GOD'S WILL

Speaking from personal experience, Chuck and Nancy share the details of their own devastating "night season"-- bankruptcy, the loss of their home and friends, a 6.8 earthquake under their rented home, and finally, the unexpected death of their son. They not only tell their own story, but go on to explain why God allows times like these and what we are to do in them.

Additional Resources:

Textbook
Personal Application Workbook
DVD Series (7 Sessions)
DVD Bible Study Package
Leader's Guide
CD Audio
MP3 Audio

1-866-775-KING

On the Internet:
http://www.kingshighway.org

What is the King's High Way?

The King's High Way is a ministry dedicated to encouraging and teaching Christians how to "walk out" their faith. Our passion is to focus on the practical application of Biblical principles. Learning how to really love as Jesus loved; how to renew our minds so our lives can genuinely be transformed; and how to develop authentic, unshakable faith throughout our night seasons. Scripture says we are to prepare ourselves for Christ's soon return. (Isaiah 62:10)

For more information, please write to:

The King's High Way Ministries, Inc.
P.O. Box 3111
Coeur d'Alene, ID 83816

or call:

1-866-775-KING

On the Internet:
http://www.kingshighway.org